View through your picture window

View through your picture window

FIVE MINUTES A DAY WITH
Charlotte Edwards

HAWTHORN BOOKS, INC.
W. Clement Stone, Publisher
New York

Library of Congress Catalog Card Number: 74–33592
ISBN: 0–8015–8314–4
1 2 3 4 5 6 7 8 9 10

Contents

View through your picture window

❧ 1 ❧

YOUR PICTURE WINDOW

In many, many of today's homes—because of the gardens, the patios, the far-reaching views of rivers and bay, mountains or sea—there is a great, wide expanse of glass known as the picture window.

There is, however, for all of us, another kind of picture window. It is more subtle, more hidden, and infinitely more important.

You see—and you all know—this has been a rugged, powerful, frightening era into which we were born. The tag end of the wild twenties, the deep end of the depression, the sharp terror of the Second World War, the scrabbling to find our feet again, the atom bomb, Korea, the confused tragedy of Vietnam, the discrediting of our government—all with so much hatred everywhere around the world! We've had to hang onto our hats and run with the wind to keep up with it all.

Sometimes the window of our thoughts, our emotions, our forward looking, grows smudged indeed.

A few years ago something happened to me. Middle age was part of it. Taking stock was another part. I looked in the mirror and really saw myself. I looked at the world and really saw *it*. And I began to wonder—a woman sort of wonder.

I wondered what, as a woman, I had really accomplished. As a woman, I wondered what lay ahead for those I loved and for the land I loved, and for the world. I wondered, above all, what had sustained me, kept me working, and

1

kept me feeling that life, no matter what it dished out, was eminently worthwhile. And so the search for my personal picture window began.

It took a long while and a great deal of digging. But when I was through, I knew that we are all together in this age! Some of us are very young. Some of us are in the warm, productive space of life. Some of us are noting the first gray in the hair. Some of us are moving more slowly, a little achy in the bones. Some of us lie quietly, most of it done and over.

You and I—and all the others like us—no matter the number of years set upon us, have one need we all share. That is a place to *look*—a personal picture window—from the *Inside* of our home, and ourselves, outward to the world.

We are tired. We are afraid. We do not know where to look. The backward glance and the forward all too often turn rancid the taste of the moment, the here and the now.

Somewhere, over the years since we were children, the doors we used to walk through freely, the windows we used to look out of together into each other's hearts and minds, have been shut, one after the other, against us. We are lost to each other in this age of movement and surface, speed and fear. Lost, and afraid to talk of anything that lies deep and meaningful within us.

Yet, it need not be like this. *If* we find a place to look. More, if we find a *way* to look. And above all, as now, if we talk together freely and intimately.

And so, in this little book, let us take just five minutes from each of our busy days to refresh ourselves and to restore our perspective. Believe me, please, it's worth trying.

✇ 2 ✇

BABY WATCHING

Did you ever stop to think how very much you—and I, of course—and all the rest of us can learn by watching a baby? Watching a small child? It seems to me it's something worth talking about.

Let's pretend a little.

You watch a baby. He is six months old—round as a milk-weed puff and as soft. He sits on a blanket on the floor by the davenport. He stretches small clutching hands for a hold on the tight material.

He pulls his apple rear upward. He stands. For a triumphant, uncertain moment he stands!

Then he drops back, knees like rubber, with a thud. Bewilderment shadows his face. He pushes the shadow back with the curve of his smile and the firming of his chin.

He reaches small clutching hands for a hold. He pulls upward. We watch a child learn to roll over, to sit up, to stand, at last to walk. We think of many things. We think of the cake that failed and the recipe that was never tried again. We think of the neighbor who snubbed a first friendly overture and whom we snub first forever again. We think of the knitting with the wool all tangled and the project dropped. We think of more important things begun, worked at, given up.

Perhaps we have stopped trying to pull our minds up from a squatting position. Perhaps it's been a long time since we have made our minds stand straight and proud and walk ahead with a new thought.

Looks. Faith. Friends. Church. Husband. Reading. Dreams. Devotion. Cooking. Housework. Which ones are failing for lack of trying?

Adult wisdom is all right, I think, in its place. But as the years run along, adults tend to let slip from their lax fingers many successes, many joys, that might have been theirs if they had just clutched one more time—pulled upward one more time.

We watch a baby. "So much to learn," we think with that adult wisdom. "Poor darling. So much to learn." And we yearn a little.

But we know, just the same, that he will be all right. He will learn to stand without hanging on. Because it never occurs to him not to try again, over and over, until what was hard becomes easy.

There is a drive in him—a force. There is a compulsion that insures his ultimate victory. The same force is in us, no matter what our age. It is hidden under the known disappointments, the laziness that is a part of us all. But it's there, flabby, unused, but waiting.

We watch a baby. The first thing we know he'll be walking all by himself. And so can we—if we keep at it and try even half as hard as he does!

❧ 3 ❧

DO THOUGHTS HAVE WINGS?

Once I knew a man whose name was Maury—a fine, gentle man who was an alcoholic and whose proudest feat was to wait till work was over to have that first drink. When he was sober, he had some interesting ideas.

Maury put together the first transmitter of the radio

station, for which we both worked, with "parts from the five and dime." He kept it working in the early days until there was enough money for him to create the fine modern transmitter of his dreams, which put the station on the map.

Maury felt, in that time before television, that TV would not succeed, because who could get sound over the mountains? Just as I, a script writer and actress, felt that it would fail, because "who was ever going to memorize a play just for one performance after all the years of script reading in radio plays?"

Well, we were both proven wrong with a vengeance.

Maury had another idea, too, that has haunted me off and on all the years since then. He thought that, if we could only tune them in, all of the voices since time began were lying in wait in the air. That if we had the right channels we could hear Lincoln's Gettysburg address, or the cries of the people going down on the *Titanic*, or Patrick Henry's "Give me liberty or give me death," or Christ's Sermon on the Mount. The whole bit, whatever anybody said anywhere at any time. If we could only hit the proper frequencies.

Well, I don't know. It's fanciful. But it doesn't seem much stranger than walking across the room, turning a button and a dial, and having color pictures and voices and faces join us whenever we choose, does it?

The other night when I couldn't sleep I thought about Maury and how he slammed into an abutment, drunk, and killed himself when he was only thirty-four. Then I thought about his hidden voices of history in the air. One thought led to another, and finally I asked myself a question. If voices can lie caged for years, how about thoughts? Are they alive and permanent somewhere in the atmosphere? Can they fly from one person to another, or do they just clog the area of space, or do they lie dead in the ground like the bodies who once thought them?

It sort of scared me, realizing all the truly evil thoughts that preceded the truly evil acts of my own lifetime alone.

5

It's probably a silly theory. But it's one to take heed of, whether it could be true or not. And, it could be a springboard to a changed attitude. To a changed world?

If thoughts have wings—even if they don't—how important it is for you and I to think enough good ones to counteract the bad thoughts that fill the world.

In my town there is a radio station that does nothing but answer phone calls and listen to people's opinions. It is somehow shocking, if you listen for any length of time, the bitterness, the hatred, the whining, the deprecation, the revenge, the misery, the hopelessness that the people in our town are eager to share with any listening ear.

Once in a great while an anonymous voice comes on and says, "Isn't this a beautiful day?" Or another asks, "Why doesn't anybody stop to appreciate some of the right things which are happening around here?" But they are lost in the melee of complaints, and nobody seems to hear them.

"As a man thinketh in his heart, so is he," says the Bible. We don't have to be Pollyannas with everything "just simply lovely." We don't have to be Coue's chanting, "Everyday in every way I'm getting better and better." We don't even have to be Dale Carnegies or like the book *The Magic of Believing* or (forgive me, Dr. Peale) the constant *Power of Positive Thinking.*

But if we can look for the good once in a while, if we send out thoughts of love to those around us, could they, as Maury believed about the voices of the past, could they just possibly have power? Could they possibly help to heal some wounds in the world, counteract the evil in the world, bring to light some hidden good in people known as bad?

No matter if they last or not, I've made a resolution. I'm going to send out at least two hearty healthy thoughts a day, whether or not, like Cock Robin's, they are arrows that "fall to earth, I know not where."

◆§ 4 §◆

THE BLESSING LIST

I have a Blessing List. Do you?

Yesterday morning I woke up before anybody else. Barefooted and night-shirted—little red hearts all over the gown and lace ruffles at the wrists, courtesy my son on my birthday—I sneaked the door open and went out for the paper.

The grass was wet and cool against my arches. Miracle and joy, the air was clear with no essence of smog. Over the rooftop of the house across the street, the sun pushed itself, as lazy as a yawn, into my sight.

I picked up the paper and dangled it and looked for once. Really looked. Calm little street. Clean little lawns. Neat little trees. Shut little doors. And quiet sky over it all.

I thought, or it was said to me as clear as this morning air: *"You'll never have it better than this. At the moment safe healthy sleepers are inside your home. At the moment your breath is pulling strong in your lungs. Utilities and house taxes are paid on time for once. Now, this moment, you are alive in full. Now, this moment, there are no planes loaded with death and headed toward this hushed little street in this hushed little city. You will never have it better than this."*

For all of yesterday, dawn until midnight, there was no restlessness in me. I tasted yesterday. I chewed it slowly and digested it sweetly. It rested easy on my tongue and in my heart.

I wish every day could be like that, don't you?

Well, of course, every day can't be. Unless we are completely insensitive to the world which extends beyond our own. But we *can* try to count out those blessings a little, can't we? Each of us has to make his own list.

7

Of course, of course, we want to be of as much help to that outside world as we can. But sometimes, some rare times—after all of the terrible news broadcasts, the confusion of thinking, the feeling of nightmare that is that world—sometimes we need to take an inner breather. To spend a day or so with a sort of shell around us, to protect us against our intense caring. We need, because our hearts are cracked and splintered every twenty-four hours on the hour, to keep the circumference of our emotions within the fence of our own backyard once in a while. We just can't afford, always and always, to spread ourselves thin and mourning for the whole wide universe. Maybe, who knows, those hundreds of thousands who inhabit our mental hospitals did just that.

So, there must be—for you, for me—the refresher. The day of the Blessing List, the day of being healthily selfish. Just for a little while. Just until we get a second wind, a second strength, a second courage.

ᵉᔆ 5 ᵇᵉ

WHAT ABOUT WORK?

I knew a woman once who considered it a big job just to get up in the morning. Facing a sink adorned with breakfast dishes for two people, she would sigh and moan, "Work, work, always work."

I always felt sorry for that woman who suffered whenever there was anything to do that wasn't purely pleasure. It seems to me as if her daily bread must have been pretty flat. It seems to me that work is like yeast, and—if our lives are to be light and fluffy, flavorful, filled with good texture—work itself is the only leavening that will stir it, bubble it, make it lift.

On my desk I have a large sign. It reads: "If you want to kill time, try working it to death."

I think about that, and it's like a spur. Nobody really wants to *kill* time, but rather just to use it, to grab hold of it as it speeds by.

I've read quite a few things about work, too, most of them said by Anon., that famous old fellow.

"Hard work is an accumulation of easy things you didn't do when you should have." We all know that on cleaning day, don't we?

And somebody once said: "I am a great believer in luck. The harder I work, the more of it I seem to have."

And somebody else said, on the debit and cynical side: "Work hard and save your money. Then, when you're old, you can have all of the things which only young people can enjoy."

And, seriously, George Bernard Shaw said: "I want to be thoroughly used up when I die. For the harder I work, the more I live. Life is no brief candle for me. It is a sort of splendid torch which I have got hold of for the moment—and I want to make it burn as brightly as possible, before handing it on to future generations."

My father wasn't any Shaw. But he always said to me: "Kid, the one thing in life which will never let you down is work. It always gives back to you exactly what you give to it."

He believed it too. He died suddenly one night. Moments after he was gone, I went into the kitchen. On the littered table were two radios he was repairing. Both of them had little inner lights going, being tested so that he could finish the job early in the morning.

Our six-year-old son, when told of his grandfather's death, looked up at me and said, "I bet Bumpa is very busy in heaven."

I asked him, "Doing what, Tom?"

And he said, "Sweeping off the stars for God."

It made me feel better. Even in heaven my father wouldn't want to float idly about on a golden cloud. Work!

≈§ 6 §≈

WHO SPEAKS FOR GOD?

When I was young I talked a great deal. Articulate, they call it nowadays. My mother used to say, probably exhausted by my constant chatter, "Still waters run deep." Perhaps because she reminded me of it so often I found myself attracted to quiet people. You know, the kind who are always there, seeming to watch and listen, their eyes speaking, while you splash your thoughts and ideas into busy sentences. I read all sorts of powerful thoughts into the quiet face that nodded instead of spoke.

After a while, of course, I discovered that most people who have something to say *say* it. And finally I sort of gave up on quiet people, accepted their silence, and felt most of them were pretty shallow.

I was reminded of this acceptance last week when we—my husband and I—took along for a day's ride the little girl next door.

Lindy is eight—going on forty. She is blonde and loving and has adopted us, much to our pleasure. She thinks a lot, and sometimes we are hard put to answer her questions.

She stared out the window of the back seat, not wiggling as much as usual. She "claimed" cows and horses and trees as "hers," and I let her count more than I did.

She was quiet for a long time; then she asked a question. "Why," she said slowly, "Nonny, when you talk to God, why doesn't he talk back to you?"

I thought about it for a few miles. Finally I felt almost ready for her.

Who speaks for God? The ultimate Quiet One? Unlike the

quiet people, never shallow, always deep? Christ, yes. But what—who—else? That an eight-year-old can understand?

Can she understand this? If I say: "Lindy, last summer we all went to the county fair, the old-fashioned one. Remember the building filled with birds. There was a pheasant—black on white. But such fine-lined black, such a perfect pattern moving symmetrically down the wings, across the back, up to the matching beak. There were doves and pigeons, and around their necks were heavy threads of sequins that outshone any of man's conniving. In the animal barn there was a fat, clean mother pig with fourteen small babies fighting for her nourishment. And ponies and horses, each one different from its neighbor, each one perfectly marked and with alive, soft eyes.

"Miracle upon miracle—and the voice of God.

"Once a few years ago, in a pour-down rain, we spied a kitten on our roof. It was no bigger than my hand, and every delicate rib showed from its starving. We had a cat. No more cats, my husband said. But he set a ladder and climbed to rescue the bit of soaking fluff.

"It took ten days to get the kitten to come to me, moving food closer each day. When it did, I carried it into the house and gave it to our older cat. He immediately began to wash the kitten. He showed it where the food and water were. He curled around it at night and kept it warm. They were inseparable, and the older cat led the way protectively always until he died. For a long time the young cat was lost and grieving without him.

"Love among the smallest. A word from the Lord.

"There is that court behind us, Lindy, and in the wintertime, you know, it is a white bleak expanse studded with bare limbs of trees and bushes. And in the summer, it is wide shade and great fat round bushes of hydrangeas. To sit in the backyard is to look over the climbing rose bushes on our fence, which were nothing but tangled twigs through the cold months, to see the glory of full blooming.

11

"Death and rebirth. God.

"There is this ride we are taking. All around us are hills, almost mountains, and every one of them is blazing in the sun with the myriad colors of autumn.

"Who speaks, child?

"There is the shell picked up on the beach and the driftwood. There is the fine sand and the waves that move tentatively in and out, ruffed with white foam. There is, with no fear in you, the momentous skyward excitement of a thunderstorm.

"Not just the eyes. The ears, too. Your laughter, Lindy. A fragment of a whistling boy's tune. The rustle of wind through heavy trees. The bubble of a creek over rocks."

Can she understand that eyes and ears and taste and touch and smell—all speak for God? We count them out. Not among the manmade frenetic world of pollution, but searching for the repetitive, the constant, the eternal, the never-changing world that speaks for God. Speaks softly, yes, but so consistently that we sometimes, often, take it for granted—and never should.

I'm ready to tell her. But she changes the subject. She puts a hand on my gray hair. "I love you, Nonny," she says. She promises, "When you and Gubby are really old and can't take care of yourselves, I will come and give you food in bed and keep the house clean."

And I don't say anything, caught as I am in the thought, "You too, child. You with your caring and compassion. You speak for God."

⋖ 7 ⋗

THE BAND STILL PLAYS

The trouble with having a little age on you—well, one of them anyway—is that you know contrast breaks the heart—and sometimes the will. Ever think of that?

As recently as our childhood, this was a forward-moving land. People believed in America. They stood with hands on hearts, hats off, as the flag went by, and they rose as one to sing "The Star-Spangled Banner." It wasn't corn to love your country, to believe in its basic precepts.

Once upon a time, it wasn't corn either to feel that Horatio Alger had "something there." A man, any man, in America could start low, work hard, get himself an education, better his status, set his own horizons, and move toward them steadily, searching out himself on the way.

Once it wasn't "square" to pray—publicly, privately, anywhere it hit you, admitting a Power beyond yourself.

When the middle-aged American was young, he wasn't some kind of a "nut" if he believed in virtue and its own reward. He set his own standards, unimpaired and uninfluenced by his neighbors, and tried to bring up his kids accordingly.

Once we knew that we had only *one* life, and how we lived would lead us into old age in pride and with character.

Well, today the band still goes marching down the street, flag flying, or that flag is pulled down slowly against a sunset. A lump-in-the-throat experience for those who are middle aged.

But today we're frankly running scared from the crackpots on the far-far left and the far-far right, who have done their best—or worst—to make suspect, to undermine, to ridicule everything we believe in.

And who's got the nerve to say to anybody and everybody: "I love America. I would die for my country"?

Middle-aged eyes get clouded. Not cataracts. Just shock at change. For a quarter century we've watched and listened and, good obedient children, used up our youth and first strengths doing what we were told.

Middle aged—yes—and the middle class. That's us. The salt of the earth, the solid center of the country. Not the wealthy, to move with assurance and power. Nor the poor, to be pitied and financed. Not the evil. Nor the saints.

13

We are the gray mass, you and I, the steady, the plodding, the norm, the average. All right! We are also the heartbeat and the lifeblood of America, and there are a heck of a lot of us.

It is not too late for us to do something for this country.

Me, I don't know a single answer. Me, I've got just about enough steam left to build a bomb shelter. But instead, I think I'll stand up and be counted and put my hand on my heart as the band goes by, flag flying! And open my mouth and sing out: "I love America. I would die for my country. But it's high time I began to *live* for it!"

ℴℂ 8 ℂℴ

REWEAVING

Do you ever take a moment to read the classified section of your paper? Now there is something to stare at. I found an ad the other day that read: "Dress alterations, all kinds. Reweaving good as new. Skirts shortened."

And I got to thinking about skirts, or the lack of them.

Once, and not very long ago, remember, they started at a clipped-in waist and blossomed like full flowers into a ripple of petals under which were half a dozen petticoats with lace! And now look! Why, just the other day I heard that mini skirts are out and micro skirts are in, and they're creating some sort of riot in France, which is perfectly understandable. I don't want to sound prejudiced, but honestly, I ask you, outside of those of tiny tots did you ever see a pair of knees, male or female, front or back view, that were attractive? Anyhow, to get back to that classified ad. The business of "Reweaving" and "Skirts shortened" got into my mind and stayed there. And pretty soon it had words,

14

although I'm no poet. Not by a million miles. But this is what I thought:

> You can say whatever you like
> But I'll never believe it's true
> That a dress which is made over
> Is as good as one that's brand new!
> A friendship ripped seamwise, then patched,
> Has a bad time fitting again.
> A love affair split, then re-welded,
> Leaves holes for mistrust's chilly rain.
> It's better sometimes to start fresh.
> A new friend, a new love, new lace.
> It's really quite easy to do—
> Except in the case of an old, tired face,
> An old tired heart, which can't bear a fresh start,
> But treasures the dress, the friend who's a mess,
> The love that hurts, and longer skirts!

Well, at least it gives us something to look forward to, and I have a closet full of dresses with calf-length hems that I'm not going to do a *thing* to.

A real poet friend of mine, Ethel Jacobson, believes that it's better to start fresh with new dresses too. Only she has a little quibble with some of them. She writes about such a fresh frock: "It looked so different on the dummy, Without my derriere and tummy!"

And as long as we're talking about clothes today and seem in a poetic mood, may I share with you one of my favorite verses, again written by a California friend, Elizabeth Ellen Long, who says:

> God bless all brave old ladies
> Bent of back and lame,
> Who come to church in their Sunday-best,
> Lest they should cause Thee shame.

Bless them, keep them, everyone,
The gallant, long-since fair,
Who, calling on Thee in Thy house,
Choose pretty clothes to wear.

I like that. Don't you?

꧁ 9 ꧂

PRIME RIBS AND RHUBARB PIE

One night a while back, I wanted to start all over. I wanted to be young again and live in two rooms and keep them shining. Did you ever feel like that?

I wanted to buy, when the baby was coming, a big monster of a house that needed paint and paper, that cost little down and less a month, and that had a small lot that needed no special tending. I wanted to be leisurely and patient with the hands stretched out to me.

You see, the other night I lay awake in the dark, deeply content for all my asking. I asked myself, and now I ask you: "Where does a woman's first and greatest fulfillment lie? Where is her surest satisfaction?"

The day of the night of my thinking, I was home, and ambition rode supreme in me. Now I am familiar with ambition. But this was different, a kind not often allowed to come to the surface, because not often is there *time* for it.

I hemmed bathroom curtains. I went to the store and bought rhubarb and spent almost two hours concocting a pie. I set the table, ignoring the TV trays, brought out candles, found flowers, and started the fire in the fireplace.

Then, I corralled everybody, taking my time, speaking softly instead of snapping at them because I had so much to do.

We all took our time. The candles winked, and the flowers tossed perfume. The prime rib offered a variety from dark crusty brown to oozing red. The pie was perfect.

Eventually everybody in my family seemed to want to kiss or pat me!

That night, I, who have worked all my grown years, knew something, one way or another. If I could do it over again, I would be a housewife, a mother, a daughter, a wife, and *nothing else*. In all areas of my young life, I would take *time* for the slow cooking, the slow basting of life's pleasures, the slow browning of life's growing, everything turned to low heat and steady and sure and watched.

You see, that evening my ill mother called me into her room and told me how kind I was to her. The boy, snug in his bed, put in his call too. I sat beside him, and it all began to come out—the friends, the worries, the great unreal and unrealized dreams. Later, my husband sat down beside me on the davenport and pushed my head gently against his shoulder and held me in silence.

No wonder I went to bed so happy I couldn't sleep! Everything I wanted from each of them, all of them, like the juices in that prime rib, came out to me. Because I cooked a good meal!

No. Not that, alone. I cook quite a few of them, really. But I don't do it with slow-paced timing. I don't hum a satisfied tune as I work. I don't do it joyfully, in no hurry and with affection, for a pie, a candle, a place setting, and *them*.

That day with all of the proper ingredients mixed in proper proportion shines in my memory—a day of tasting, of value, of nourishment, of beauty. When I think of it, I think, "This is the day which the Lord hath made."

I hope I don't ever forget it.

ᴥᶀ 10 ᶋᴥ

THE OLD WATCHMAN

When I was sixteen, there was a tiny cubicle of a house for the watchman at the railroad crossing on our way home from school. Whenever we passed, he waved to us. The flicker of a pot-bellied stove colored the little dirty window and made a sort of warmth around him.

One Christmas, the sixteenth year of my life, I got a kind of religion. I wanted to do something for somebody who didn't expect it. I bought woolen gloves and a scarf and made fudge. I wrapped the whole thing in bright paper with a big bow. When my mother and I went delivering packages, I stopped at the little crossing house.

The old watchman opened the door. He smiled at me, and I couldn't see any teeth at all in the pool of his mouth.

I said "Merry Christmas" and shoved the package at him.

The knuckles of his hands were big and red. I was glad about the gloves.

He hefted the package, let his mouth close, and suddenly his eyes were there for me to see. What can I say about those eyes—warmth, dark depths, childish joy? Not when it's an old man in a crossing house, with the smell of his stove and the smell of himself reaching out to pollute clean Christmas air. Besides, how are you going to say that the earned wrinkles of his face were in his eyes? That sounds silly. But they matched—as if he'd been given a wrinkle and a facet of light for every single thing he'd known of happiness and its opposite.

I smiled uncertainly and hurried back to the car. There I heard him call. "Wait," he cried, looking like a black matchstick as he stumbled on the slick highway. He reached me and fumbled his hand toward me. What was in it he tucked into my hand. I had trouble holding still. When you are young, you are conscious of age, of "tomorrow we die."

"Merr' Christmas," he said. "You buy yourself somethin' nice, huh?"

I wanted to give it back but I didn't know how to, so I just said, "Yes and thank you." I got in the car. Through the rearview mirror he got blacker and thinner and older. But his hand was up, flipping like a fin the whole time.

My mother said, "Why, dear, what a lovely thing for you to do!"

I wasn't so sure; I felt that I had been topped. That my gesture had been lost somewhere in the shuffle.

Every Christmas I bought gloves and scarf and fixed candy. Every Christmas he had the dollar ready—folded into a tiny square, very dirty as if maybe it had been tucked into the greasy corner of black work pants for a long time.

I never knew his name nor where he lived, and one Christmas there was a young fat man at the crossing.

I rode right by. I didn't want the fat man to tell me what had happened to the old watchman. I knew. Just as I have known all these years since how it felt to be old beyond reckoning and not very clean, nobody to talk to except a hissing stove, and to have a dollar in my pocket to give to a girl in a big convertible.

What do you call such a feeling, my friends? What do you do to treasure such a beginning of universality? How do you protect it—so easily a part of you at sixteen—so easily and steadily and consistently leaked out of you during hard days and nights and cynicism and worry and trouble—and fear?

Universality—yes. To care—not just to sympathize—but to *be* with, to *feel* with. This is what we—not just you and I but the whole hurting millions of people, all those mourners at the graves of our assassinated great—must remember, must hold onto with a deadly grip, must increase instead of decrease or lose entirely.

19

Universality—yes. "Ask not for whom the bell tolls, it tolls for thee." Yes. But above all: "And the second is like unto it. Thou shalt love thy neighbor as thyself."

◄§ 11 §►

HAPPY BIRTHDAY

Happy birthday, Somebody!

Now isn't that a silly way to begin our time together? But surely, somewhere, there must be one of you who awakened this morning, a little heavy with the knowledge that you were a year older. Right?

A year older? Of course not, you're just twenty-four *hours* older than you were yesterday, Somebody. And you know, you can turn the whole thing over, like a piece of money with two shining sides, and be *glad* to have a birthday. Yes, you can. All you have to do is to thank whatever powers that be that you've, in these frantic, troubled times, survived another three hundred and sixty-five days.

Something that happens to me on birthdays is that I miss my mother very much. I don't think this is because she gave me life, although almost all the time I'm grateful that she did. But it's because of the birthday cakes. She wasn't particularly a fancy cook, but somehow that cake with candles, on my own special day, tasted better than any other cake in the world.

A wonderful thing happened to me last year, after all the birthdays without that special feeling. (Who can teach a husband to bake a cake? Not me, anyhow, and think of all the dishes to clean up afterward!) But last year, by some sort of extrasensory perception, one of the ladies of our church knocked on our door. I imagine you have at least one like her

20

in your church—always there, always working, always agreeing to be of help where she can.

I was feeling a little sorry for myself. I don't believe in reminding people that I was born, at least not on a certain day, and the mail had brought no cards at all. Then—that knock. There she was—white hair, broad smile, and hands loaded with the biggest whitest coconuttiest cake I'd seen since my mother died.

I didn't just cry, I bawled. Scared her, too, and she ran off like a rabbit.

Anyhow, to get back to you, Somebody, whomever you are with a birthday today, I wrote a poem for you myself. And bless you.

There was a time when we were young and gay and light, unthinking,
When we could face a Natal Day with smiles and gaze unblinking;
When to mark up another year was something to be proud of
And celebrate and tell them all and rooftop shout aloud of!

But time goes by and years add up and wrinkles dent and grace declines,
And it's no help to hear them say that birthdays are like vintage wines.
No, it's no help to count the days and know the ones remaining
Are fewer than the ones we've known, and meet them uncomplaining.

And yet, dear friends, a thing is so, whatever wild depression,

It's good to have weathered another one in the process of succession.

It's good to count the aches and pains and know they've been defeated.

It's good to count the pleasant hours however rarely meted.

One other thought, for what it's worth,
From where I've always stood,
No matter *which* the birthday, dear,
On you it sure looks good!

⊷§ 12 §⊶

LOVE'S MANY FACES

I think today about love, and the lovers of life and people.

A while back when the hippie movement was at its crest, young people walked the streets and handed out flowers and cried, "Love!"

What did they mean by it?

Did they have the vaguest idea of people who are all lovers—as my family was? Lovers of life, lovers of hope. No matter what happened to them, they thought love, talked love. Whatever they pedestaled their lives on, my family, love was a sort of cement that held everything together. Country, the world, the churches, the people one unto another.

It is not easy to come from the womb of such love out into any world, certainly not the one that surrounds us all at this long later time. The umbilical cord never seems to be cut somehow, and no matter what, the blood flows from the mother source, so wrapped in flexible but sturdy membrane that whatever attacks it, at any age, the love keeps bubbling through, a substance in itself, which cannot be dammed.

Now is now for all of us. And it is hard to search your own "love" earliness when you're absorbed in the "hate" of today. Or know the value of any of your life except that it has created some courage and much caring.

What is there left for us except to accept the day and try to be one with the present?

To be one with the present is to note the breath as it is drawn. The wind as it blows or the sun or rain or snow or fog as it offers itself.

As I think this and look out of my window, there is, shimmering through the yard, a very small, very busy, very bright yellow butterfly. It does not know that the sun, this November day, is as evanescent as its wings and promises only death to the bushes it flits to. How fortunate, too, that very small yellow butterfly on an Indian summer day. Nowhere in its pin head, its thready feelers, exists the knowledge of imminent death, which even the frantic squirrels flashing past each other in a great last-minute rush know with such sure instinct, such remembered experience. The awareness of the finish, the climax and the goneness do not belong to the butterfly.

So, shivering its wings in a kind of morning ecstasy, trying to rival the clear gold of the sun as if it were a fluttering remnant scissored from that orb, the butterfly is sad only to the one who watches him—the wise passing geese, the small hurrying birds, always the squirrels and the human being.

All of those who know better, who read the book inexorably to the end word and shut it with blind finality, all of those who are so wise in the foreknowing see the butterfly and sigh, each in his own fashion, for the foolishness that lives in the moment.

But that sigh is foolishness too. From the depths of all the unaware moments, the times when we, like the butterfly, held no sense of death and carried eternity within us—those moments are the butterfly that flutters inside of us all and has its time and knows all the tomorrows that emerged from the yesterdays.

And I think: "The love and the butterfly must never die within us, not being remembered, not being treasured. Or we are all truly lost."

⋖ 13 ⋗

KIDS—BLESS 'EM

You know something? In all the years of my good long life, I've never held enough babies. Not only ones of my own, but nieces and nephews and neighbors'. Nor have I, although I've known a lot of them, talked with little children, middle children, and growing-up children enough to satisfy me.

Kids are wonderful at any age, aren't they? Did you have to go through, for instance, those long, hard, and—let's face it—expensive years of having one of your youngsters wear braces? We did. For what seemed like forever.

But the day finally came when the doctor took those darned things off, and his nurse did a very, very thorough job of cleaning—and lo—a mouthful of straight, white pearly teeth was suddenly shining out from a young happy face.

We had a celebration for the unveiling at our house. And then, off shot the remade young man, to show the world his beauty. Me, I sat down at my faithful typewriter, and a silly little rhyme came out. I share it with you now.

> Today he had his braces off
> And what was smirk became a smile,
> And what was silver turned to white,
> Young ladies to beguile.

Today he brushed his stubby hair
And shined his best black shoes.
He even clipped his fingernails
And ran to grin the news.

Which adds itself to the fact that before dancing class way back there one night, my husband discovered a razor, full-fledged, on the rim of the washbowl. He yipped.

"You didn't? he cried. "Not yet. Not that fuzz above the lip. You'll start something you can't stop."

Scorn in the eyes, the very young dancing man said, all groomed and ready, "Course not, Dad. You crazy? I just wanted to cut a piece of string."

His father let go with a relieved sigh.

"I'll tell you something, though," the boy went on, dead serious. "You know Tim? Yeah. Well, Tim shaves every single, solitary—month!"

Imagine!

Which in turn reminds me of my niece at about age six, who, when I was deep in conversation with her mother and a guest, kept pulling on my skirt. "Auntie," she kept saying over and over.

I turned my adult look on her. "Jan," I said severely, "don't you know you're not supposed to interrupt when grown-ups are talking?"

She let go of my skirt and began to turn away. "That's just the trouble," she said mournfully. "Grown-ups are *always* talking." A truth, indeed, out of the mouths of babes.

Richard Armour writes a lot of verses about kids, sometimes with exasperation. He says:

Grade school is properly named, we feel.
But little our cause for boasting.
For the grade is UP, and the grade is REAL.
And our son has a way of coasting.

He also sometimes seems to want to hurry things a bit. He writes:

> Get in and study, Junior, please,
> And skip a grade or two.
> Though I'm not fond of prodigies,
> I cherish your I.Q.
> Obey the teacher, break no rule,
> And speed the blessed day
> When you will graduate from school—
> And I from P.T.A.

I'll bet you have a few to contribute, too, don't you? Oh well, it's good to remember such sayings, especially when the kids are no longer kids but all wise and grown and finished off at the edges, isn't it?

⋖§ 14 §⋗

GOODBYE, FEAR

You know, to deal with anything—from an ingrown toenail to a bleeding ulcer—you have to know *first* what you are dealing with. You can't treat the toenail by ignoring it and pretending it doesn't hurt. You can't feed the ulcer raw onions because you refuse to acknowledge it exists. And it's the same way with fear.

It seems to me that the first thing any of us can do and must do, today, is to admit that fear lives. In *us* and in the *world*. And having admitted it, do something about it. How, you ask, and I don't blame you for the question.

Men on a battlefront know the enemy, are trained to cope with him, realize it's kill or be killed, and have plenty of ammunition to accomplish victory. We, we little ones, do not have this concentrated incentive as a group or as individuals. And we have to manufacture our own ammunition.

Mine—if I may be personal, and there's no other way for me to be—is a sort of daily pledge. I make it to God or to myself or to those I love or to humanity in general. I'm not sure which. But it goes something like this.

I say: "I will not fear today." It is a promise made to show my faith. To whatever great Power there is, but it is also and equally a promise to myself. So that for the hours and minutes ahead of me I can move forward among my tasks and friends and those I love.

What a difference it makes, not being afraid. The ache in the shoulder, the pain in the chest, the weariness of the body, are not added up like fool's gold. The state of the world, making again and again its ancient and horrible mistakes, becomes a matter of prayer rather than a sudden shrinking of the heart and trembling of the mind. With fear erased, there is room for something better to grow and a fresh page on which to write my day.

It would be fine if on that page there could be no mistakes, nothing crossed out or scribbled or misspelled. Just a perfect page, one perfect day, in a succession of blotted, crumpled ones. I am not so wise as that, nor so foolish as to think I can accomplish it.

But if I do not fear, I at least have the *page* on which to try. So, like the alcoholic who makes a daily promise of abstinence, I pledge that today, with help, I will touch no fear.

It helps. It really does. Just to have your mind going around and around in circles of deep worry, to watch the news tragedies on TV and be lost and gone in depression for a day, to catch always the dark note and have it become your only melody, is to drag yourself and your family and those around you into a blackness which can lead to mental illness. Or, on the other hand, to pretend there's nothing to be afraid

27

of, like a child chanting, "You can't scare me, you can't scare me," becomes a kind of illness, too.

So—there is the morning pledge, which admits fear exists but refuses to be intimidated. Try it sometime?

⋞ 15 ⋟

THESE ARE MY JEWELS

I heard a little story last week. It was about a church circle, a large group of women who were "very well off." In their midst, with nobody knowing exactly how she got there, was a younger woman in her early thirties.

Everybody liked the younger woman in our story, although her clothes were simple and even a little shabby. She had a small smile and a quiet voice, and she always seemed to have such a good time at the meetings.

At the beginning of the fall season, as usual, the president of the circle asked for volunteers to offer their homes for luncheon meetings. Before anybody could speak up, the young woman said, "I'd be proud if you would come to my house next time."

They accepted, of course. There was a certain amount of buzzing among them about what to expect. They were right, too.

The house was on the outskirts of town. It was very small and even shabbier than the young woman. They had to huddle and push and sit on uncomfortable, borrowed chairs and hold plates in their laps.

But it turned out, somehow, to be the best meeting they'd had in a long time.

The young woman was radiantly happy to have them. She greeted them with such pride and graciousness that it didn't matter there were only dollar throw rugs on the floor and not enough cups.

What mattered was that her husband, who worked nights, came through the back door fresh from playing in the park with three children so beautiful everybody gasped.

What mattered was that the young woman excused herself and brought out from the bedroom a baby with enormous brown eyes, an enormous smile, and a gurgle, who let himself be happily passed around from one strange lap to another.

The older woman who told me about it sat in my living room. When she moved, the diamonds on her fingers shot out sparks, and the heavy silk of her dress gleamed.

"When I walked out of there," she said, looking surprised to find herself saying it, "I felt poor. I got in the new car Henry gave me for my birthday and raced home. And I didn't feel rich at all. There was something about that house—strange, isn't it?"

After she was gone, I got out my book of quotations. I found it quite easily. Robert Burton, 1577–1640.

"Cornelia kept her in talk till her children came from school, 'And these,' said she, 'are my jewels!' "

Something to meditate upon, isn't it?

⋖§ 16 §⋗

ONE WAY TO HAPPINESS

Everybody wants to be happy, of course. Most people really try to be. And many do not succeed.

Mrs. Smith lives down the street from us. She has a nice husband and two grown children. I've known her for a long time. I've never seen her happy.

Her children in the days of their growing up were always "problems," although they didn't get into any more trouble than other kids. Her husband was always "passed over" when it came time for a promotion or a raise, although he always earned more and moved upward more quickly than mine did. Her refrigerator, her car, her furniture, her rugs, her clothes, were always belittled by her because someone else she knew had more expensive ones. Although she got two of each for every one that most of the rest of us neighbors did.

She spent a good deal of time in the beauty parlor, looking at movie magazines and envying the dazzling successes of celebrities. She always seemed to hit upon, in the newspapers or the TV news, the enormous amount of money that some people have in the world. "Inherited," she used to say. Or "They married a rich man," she'd declaim and look at her husband reproachfully.

I know a lot of Mrs. Smiths—and Misters too—don't you?

I always feel sorry for them. Were they born with their heads tilted up to see those who had it better or easier or had more than they did? Did they ever tip their noses down and use their good eyes to gaze on what was beneath them?

Now, I'm not a special person in any way. But since I've been young it's been part of my inherent nature to be aware of those whose difficulties are *worse* than mine. I hardly ever seem to notice the ones who have it better. Hardly. Once in a while, maybe, when somebody who has everything the world can give him throws it all away on a dissolute life.

It's amazing how much happiness this kind of attitude can engender. Heaven knows we as a family have known some very tough times, but there was always someone who had it worse.

During that nonlamented depression when I was ringing doorbells to get people to sample newspapers in the snow—always the snow—a door was opened to me by a family not long from Britain. They lived in half of a great double house. A thin pasty little girl let me in. She invited me to come back to the kitchen.

There was absolutely no furniture in the living room or dining room. Passage through them, even after being out in the snow, was like walking through a block of ice. The kitchen was warm though, heated to the farthest corner by a great iron stove. The mother was little larger than the daughter, pert, birdlike, wrapped in an old dress too big for her and an apron that wound around twice. There was a young boy in the corner reading an old science magazine. There was a beautiful four-year-old girl hanging over the table, warily plunging her fingers into a glass of strawberry jam.

They didn't ask me my business. They all just smiled as if I were expected. The mother pulled a flat pan from the oven and skimmed off a bottom skin of wax paper from a yellow fluffy concoction.

"Eggs, we have" she said in her clipped accent, "and jam from the summer wild strawberries. So it's jelly roll for a special treat—and for supper too, as a fact. If you'll wait just a few moments, you shall share it."

I waited. Something about them drew my own story. They accepted it as they would a gift, exclaiming upon its good points, ignoring its bad. In return they gave me a restrained tale of their own difficulties.

The father in the hospital. No cash in the house for two months. Furniture sold. Landlord letting them stay because he couldn't rent the place anyhow until spring. The iron stove stayed hot and kind by means of wood the boy had cut before snowfall. Both the boy and girl had tried to find spare-time work. Almost impossible.

"Their education comes first," the mother said. "I won't have them leaving school to work even if there were work to be had. Hannah stands highest in her class. Next year, sure, she will win a scholarship."

I listened and absorbed the heat of the stove, the warmth of them. I looked at the sunshine of the jelly roll, the studded crimson of the jam. I left there regretfully, with a gift apple in my pocket. And more. Much more.

I left there with the refreshment of renewed courage, the

31

hopefulness of the little woman's "next year," the knowledge that we, our family, were one out of many. And that some people had it tougher than we did. Above all, I left there with a lightness in the inner spot that had darkened me and almost an exultation of happiness. The kind I used to feel as a child for no reason at all.

When I got "home" to the gray box of a house, owned by a widow who tolerated us in two bedrooms with kitchen privileges, warmth rushed out to meet me, and dinner was being cooked on a good modern gas stove—with meat! And there were comfortable beds waiting for us upstairs.

I was happy.

⊸§ 17 §⊷

THE SHELL AND THE KERNEL

Around Christmastime do you think of Dickens' *Christmas Carol*? I do. Of old Scrooge and the terrible way he had to face three Christmases—the ghost of Christmas past, Christmas present, and Christmas future. Let's talk about Christmas past today, shall we?

When I was young, all Christmases seemed somehow to center around my father, Santa Claus incarnate without a beard, with everything extravagant, lavish, gifts piled to the ceiling, every present on the list, every wish, bought and given.

His generosity went beyond the family, though. Before any gift was purchased for us, we went downtown as a family. Dad would look up and down the street, often through flying snow, until he found a small newsboy, in those days when they were prevalent. He'd walk over to him. "Do you believe in Santa Claus?" he'd ask gruffly. Most of the time, the scrawny weary child would shake his head. "Well, you'd better," Dad would say, "because *here he is!*"

32

Mother and I would watch him as he bought all of the boy's papers, as they disappeared together into the nearest department store. We'd go have a cup of chocolate and keep an eye on the door. When they emerged, the boy would be in new clothes from the skin out, with a heavy topcoat and cap to finish him off. His arms would be loaded with every gift he most wanted from the toy or sport department. Dad would hustle toward us before the boy could speak too much of thanks, and we'd go about our shopping. Most often the kid stood there, stunned, watching Santa disappear into the snow.

Then came the depression.

The first winter of that time I walked home from the bus, in a totally strange city, in a slow snow. In that flashing way the mind has, all the other Christmases walked with me.

I came to the gray house where we rented rooms and had the privilege of cooking. I opened the door, and there was the smell of onions and hamburger, our tradition for years, real as the light that hit me warmly in the face. There was the pine smell of that little tree in the corner of the living room, not our living room but belonging to the widow from whom we rented.

I walked in there and stood looking at it. It didn't go to the ceiling. It didn't even reach my waist. There were very few ornaments on it. But there was a string of red, green, yellow and blue lights, all winking. White tissue paper starred with false snow was crumpled under it. There was a hand-cut star on top.

I stooped down. I rested my hands on my knees. I leaned my head forward. Like a child allowed to look but not touch, I studied the presents, wrapped in red and white tissue with neat bows. I read the tags. Four tags. That was it. That was all.

The muscles of my stomach knotted like a cramp in the arch of my foot. I couldn't get my breath, and I was too weak to pull myself to my feet. I just stooped there until my knees cramped, too.

My mother's voice called from the kitchen, "That you, dear?"

Dad cried, "They're browned to a turn, kid. Get a move on."

The big old kitchen was filled with heat. It was filled with excitement.

I went over and sniffed at the frying pan. Dad stood over it like a guardian Saint Bernard. There was an apron around his middle, and Mother had tied a red bow in the forelock of his hair which usually fell over his face.

The widow was cutting butter into very thin squares. Her face looked round and younger and ironed out.

"Your folks asked me to supper," she explained. "I told them it was butting in, but they *would* have it." She looked at me questioningly.

I was almost drowned in the wave of feeling that came at me then. For all of them in the old kitchen. For us all, the first Christmas away from home, but at home still in some strange way.

That was when I realized that we had made an exchange, our depression-hit family. We had exchanged luxury, the big world, the friends, the known, the outer, for something smaller—something I sensed dimly that would very likely in the long run be richer and larger.

It was like trading a huge aquamarine for a very small emerald. It was like throwing away the shell so that you might get at the kernel. It was holding a full measure of tenderness.

It was, in a strange way, Christmas for the first time.

Do you remember a Christmas like that? To enrich your present one, whatever it may be?

I hope so.

✎ 18 ☙

SHARING GOD'S WORK

Every year, as the holidays grow nearer and as I have looked around at the women in stores, I begin to think about us and how much, sometimes, we underestimate our place in the world. Do you know, when we really study it, that most of the time we are sharing God's work just because we *are* women?

Sometimes I think that we're a little too humble. And I'm not talking of Women's Lib.

For instance, my neighbor likes to cook, especially at Christmas. She likes to have company. She works all day on dishes that are eaten in a short time, but that short time is gastronomical delight. She welcomes her guests, looking fresh and as if she hadn't hurried a bit. She has candles on the table and all of those bright pottery bowls exuding sundry teasing smells.

She brings people together as definitely as she sets the table. You can see it happen. The way strangers who don't even know each other, heartened by that food, those smells, the brightness of the decorations, grow mellow. They start with the common denominator of good eating. They invariably go on from there, making more than a delightful evening. Making friends.

My neighbor belittles her place in the scheme of things. She is in awe of poets and artists and musicians. She longs wistfully for "a little talent at anything. Anything at all!"

She doesn't see that once Christ was weary and hungry, and he came to a place, and a girl named Martha brought him food. Shyly, her head bowed and her eyes lowered.

35

Brought him food and refreshed him. So that the wisdom that was in him could be sustained. Could be said. So that he had the strength to go on to the next place and the next, until now all around the world are all the things that he taught in such a small section of the world. Perhaps it was Martha's meal that made the spread of the Gospel possible. It could be.

So, my neighbor, like Martha, is sharing God's work.

And Christmas, you know how Christmas is. We women fill the stores and juggle the pennies and put great thought and care into just the thing that Uncle Jasper will want or Aunt Minnie will be surprised with. We women spend hours with tissues and ribbons, addressing cards with little notes that will bring distant friends and relatives up to date.

We women start in November to bake the fruitcakes and rush around the week before the great date to make hundreds of cookies and pieces of candy. We women sit up late putting the last touches to a handmade apron or a handknit sweater.

Then, somehow, we find time to read the story in the Bible once again, and "Twas the Night Before Christmas" and Dickens' *Christmas Carol* to the children. We build the suspense and bring out the meaning and still manage to have enough strength left to cook a big turkey dinner for all the relatives on Christmas day.

This insistence on an outward symbol of an inward grace, of marking the anniversaries of human birth with celebration and glorifying the anniversary of divine birth—this is sharing God's work. ·

So you see? In all of these ways and in the many other activities that make us "just housewives," we are a sort of instrument of God, whether we realize it or not.

If we do realize it and approach our daily routine knowing the value of every move we make, we cannot help but attain a contentment that will increase our faith and garnish our happiness. It's a thing we can start right now with whatever little chore we have to do next.

We just say to ourselves: "I am of value to the family, the community, the town, and thus the world. I am not working alone. I am inspired in the simplest ways and used for the greatest functions."

We say, "I am sharing God's work."

And we remember what some anonymous writer said, "Not everyone can do great things, but everyone can do small things in a great way."

⋞ 19 ⋟

WHERE IS THE DELIGHT?

When I was quite young, I sat in a darkened audience one time and listened to a woman named Bea Lillie as she hunched upon a high stool and sang a song. There was utter defeat in her shoulders, and (if I remember) the way she bit slowly into an apple. The song she sang was titled "World Weary."

I didn't know then exactly what it meant, but I certainly could feel the emotion behind the simple words.

And now I know it all. As you do. Right?

To be exhausted by the weight of the outside world, to me at least, means to waken in the morning with the heaviness of yesterday still in me. Sometimes there's a bright little spark that might grow into a decent flame, but the morning paper or the morning news on radio or TV seems to blow it out quickly and definitely.

The other early evening it was as if I couldn't get my breath, so variously had the world pressed against my heart all day. So I took a walk. All by myself. Didn't even tell anyone where I was going because I didn't really know.

I moved slowly three blocks down our street toward the setting sun. I nodded to people who didn't know me and didn't nod back. A little black dog followed me, and he was a companion of sorts, although he wouldn't come near me to be petted.

I came to a corner, and I stood very still.

Across the street was a house with a rummage store in it. Next to it was a small white house which had once been brown. I sauntered across and looked in the rummage window. But I didn't see its contents. What I saw was quite different.

To go into that store, once upon a time, was to set a bell tinkling and faded draperies jangling, as hands pushed them apart and the round brass circlets on the rusted brass rod at the top clinked sharply against each other. The hands were quick, as the feet were, with mistrust of children left alone with temptation. The temptation shone in glass jars with heavy fluted tops, full of rock candy on strings, licorice babies sparked with sugar, and nuggets of anise rubies which chunked the cheeks into odd shapes and diminished so slowly that they puckered the mouth like fingertips in a long hot bath.

The store was the only place I was allowed to go from the brown house, so small I was. A matter of pride accompanied my entrance, a matter of pennies in the hand to buy from the glass jars. But above all, the pride, the joy, of moving outward alone and the almost frightening yet exciting moment when those hands, white, scrawny, pushed aside the drapes to reveal a little of the hidden darkness of a room where unknown people lived.

The other evening I walked around the side of the little house that had been brown—the TV was blaring inside so loudly nobody could hear me. I moved to the yard I had known as a child.

The single tree was gone in reality, but it grew again as I looked. Once it had leaned with its scrawny, rough gray trunk in the middle of the yard, as if trying to balance against a rough sea. When it reached above the roof of the house, amazingly, it turned widespread and luxuriant like a skinny man with a head of bushy green hair.

I used to lie on my back, flat, letting an ant tickle its way up my leg and a ladybird riffle against my neck, to stare through the head of the tree. That way the hair lost most of its solidity and bald patches of sunshine showed, skinlike, through the leaves.

Beside me the doll table with its small candy loaves of pretend bread was deserted for a time, left to collect, like chocolate dots, the ants who weren't interested in me. A small world moved under my back and against my sides, a busy world to watch, belly down, as life went on among the grasses, which could be eye level if I dropped my head and set it tight against the earth.

And I was filled with delight.

Walking slowly back homeward again, back more years than city blocks, I asked myself, "Where is the delight?"

Suddenly I knew. Abruptly I was light of foot and heart. The joy in life was contained in the child who walked in an old body. The child herself was contained in that old body.

Delight, I realized, is like God. It is always there to pull upon, to gain strength and pleasure from. *If* we reach inside for it. *If* we remember. *If* we bring forth that wonder that made a whole world when we were small. Wonder in the taste of something, anything. Wonder in the smallest thing—like ants and blades of grass.

I walked quickly, my chin up, tasting the air, seeing the trees, which almost touched each other across the old street. Feeling the way my feet went down on the pavement and my muscles pulled. Anticipating the way I would fling open the door of my home to greet those I loved. Rejoicing that they were there to be greeted at all.

Strange. Everybody I nodded to or spoke to on the way

back home nodded or smiled at me. And when I put my hand out to the small black dog, he came close and licked it.

Delight.

⤍ 20 ⤏

BOY STUDYING

Well, I'll grant you that most of the talk about young people and their homework implies that we have to take a whip and crack it around their shoulders to get them to work. But, you know, it really isn't so. Have you ever watched that teen-ager of yours bent over a desk at night, trying so hard to learn what everything is all about, when he'd so much rather be doing something else? I have. And it hurt a little.

I wanted to talk to our boy, the night I thought about how hard he was working. But it would be silly. So I wrote to him, and this is what I said.

"Boy, to watch you at your desk puts the heart upon the sleeve. Shoulders hulked, long unfinished arms cramped to small space, head bowed, eyes reaching, you pull the sentences to you.

"You open the channel of your mind and try, long hour after hour, to people it with the great somber parade of mankind's knowledge.

"The Latin words speak of another age. Yet, they tell today. Rome's rise and culture and demise are there for you to know in more than grammar. Rome is your country now. You are Caesar or gladiator or galley slave. Who can tell? But the reach of America is higher than any peak of Roman days, and nearly as lost, this moment, as the peaked danger point of downslide those dead and countless years ago.

"Boy, almost man, that English book holds a key for you five years from now or ten or all the rest. Man's thoughts, his

40

inner space, unfold before you. What you absorb of them with mental, spiritual pores, will sweat out on another era. May one day seal the peace of all the universe. Or leastly, light a candle in dark minds.

"The American history, boy, look long and well upon each page. Know strongly that for every free step you take to school and church, for each of the newspapers and books you read to find the happenings of the day, for each brave word you say in young opinion, men like you have known fear and courage, loss and humility—and death. Always death.

"Boy, to give you work to do and watch you as you try, is to give you the world. Misshapen, sorry, no great heritage, but *yours*. No longer the sad possession of the one who watches with his aging heart upon his sleeve, the sleeve turned toward the door, away from you, lest you should glimpse it and feel less manly.

"Learn well, boy. In a place where grades are never marked in black and white on paper for the reading, you must find your own honor roll. And you must know that to fail is Rome once more, and everything repeated—gone and lost.

"God help you."

◦§ 21 §◦

THE GUIDED TOUR

Like most of us, I have never traveled widely. Like most of us, I have traveled fourteen days at a time. Two weeks with pay, they call it. You too?

Two weeks with pay. All through the years they form a parade of oases in the huddled, dry routine of the other fifty weeks each year. Each one spreads long with the experience

41

of space—the great rare feeling of nothing to do but look, the unexpected rising of the heart, the frightened knowledge of self's smallness.

That is what a vacation means, isn't it? That—and more.

Leisure, time to be your best and most rested self, is a commodity of great value. It has always seemed a waste to have these separate vacations. A wrong to use the only free time of the year away from those you love the most.

All the other weeks, a husband and wife have from each other only the odd, tired, used moments of the end of the day. They go into each other's arms all too often filled to the heart with weariness, with worries large and small, with the hidden threat of an early-clanging alarm clock.

All the other weeks, the children sit at the dinner table, the racing day heavy in their legs and the lids of their eyes—homework waiting on the kitchen chair, frustration their daily portion—and eat too fast and speak of nothing that they feel.

All the other weeks, they have from their parents only the necessary, viciously repetitive discipline, which is impelled by the constant awareness of an outside world into which they must be fitted and for which they must be trained.

The sad fact then remains that within the home and the family too often there just are no free hours. The end of the day—homework, dinner, dishes, baths, get-to-bed-at-a-decent-hour time—is the only shared time that remains. And it is the dregs.

Fifty weeks of the year this is so.

A vacation, for a family, can be like the honeymoon we all remember if we were fortunate enough to have had one. It can be a little time bracketed by love and by change. This change is not only of place and scenery, not only of pace. It is a deepening of attitude.

It means looking deeply at the others in the car with us and, last, at ourselves.

42

The boy has grown a great deal, hasn't he? The roundness of his cheeks flattens out. Around his firmer mouth there is a tickle of down. He has grown in other ways too. All the long year we have not had time to listen, nor he to speak. He calls the vacation a *guided tour* because things work out so well. We know that he means a guidance beyond a road map. That is a growth we had not noticed.

There is the husband. He sits at the wheel, not breaking any speed limits, not setting any goals. He whistles or sings one tune over and over. He makes small, silly jokes. He switches off the main road at any sign that intrigues us. He and the boy investigate all streams and waters.

For him there are lines we haven't observed, and tension on the mouth, and a new gray in the hair. But somehow, in that free time together, the vulnerable boy we married manages to push himself to the surface. The sight of him is all the more to be treasured, because it is so inevitable that he will soon slip back under again, drowned and lost in another hard-working year.

For the self, there is the long, straight look. The feeling of distaste for the year's mistakes, the quick temper, the sharp words, the pushing away of loving overtures, the not taking time to see all sides.

Instead of New Year's Eve, two weeks with pay is the time for resolutions. Think about it, as you turn onto the highway, with those precious fourteen days of free time ahead of you.

⋐§ 22 §⋑

MUSIC NOSTALGIA

We have a record player at our house. Had it quite a while as a matter of fact, but just recently the young added something. The square boxes—fastened at different times in

43

different places, so that wires are looped in the oddest fashion and to walk from room to room is a hazard.

Granted, stereo, whatever they call it, can be great with great music on it. We don't have much though, because it's a treasured possession of the young man who saved to buy those boxes that amplify, and it's handled very tenderly, the needle set down with great precision, each plug-in a matter of life or death. With great music it's as if we were sitting in the middle of a philharmonic auditorium surrounded by Cinamascope. Which is what we wanted.

Or did we?

According to the movie magazines I read, or scan, when my hair is drying at the beauty shop, according to the television programs I run like a rabbit to shut off whenever I'm alone and allowed to, things big and different have happened to music. Sure as shooting, something big and different has happened to musical groups and singers. Yikes!

Of course, you've heard them too—by mistake most likely, so far as TV is concerned—and seen them. Every single solitary female or male soloist has a tremolo of anywhere from three to seven notes. Every group has a resonance of fourteen stampeding elephants in a dry forest. Even with your eyes closed it's frightening. But with them open you want to find a place to hide or put a cold cloth on your head.

Naturally, you don't have to watch with the record player. You only have to listen to *one* album for three hours straight! Four LP records played clean through from the beginning to end, flipped over and played clean through again. That was an *experience*.

I survived it. And now we're all older at our house, and a lot of Bach and Chopin seem to seep around. But I know very well a lot of you are in the midst of straining to your capacity, that parental patience which always says: "Well, it could be worse. He [or she] is a good kid. No drugs. No drinking. I can stand the noise."

44

What's the matter? Have we sort of exalted our own young days? The songs that meant so much to us? I wonder. Once in a great while, there's a tribute on the air to Cole Porter or George Gershwin, or Kate Smith sings "God Bless America," and then I think we're right. There really *was* music in our day.

There was a melody line. There was a little variety and form. The arrangements were rich. Still, the beat was there. It was there, all right. And so was "Stormy Weather," "The Man I Love," "As Time Goes By," "Someone to Watch over Me," "Blues in the Night," "Two Loves Have I."

I sound like my own grandmother. I feel like her, too. She probably felt the same way about "Down by the Old Mill Stream," "When You and I Were Young, Maggie," and "My Bonnie Lies over the Ocean."

I guess I'll have to amble down to the record shop. Somewhere in the files perhaps there will be on an LP and in stereo a rich, round voice—on key; a rich, round arrangement; a rich, round composer.

The next problem will be to get my hands on that record player long enough to displace the modern noise for five or ten minutes. I could always send somebody to the store maybe, preferably a store twenty-five miles away.

You know what, though? There's a funny little modern melody that has been haunting me. Rock it some. Put words to it. "Run away, little boy, run away, little boy—"

There's a fortune in that bitter sort of commentary stuff, do you know that? Wish I knew how to play a guitar. Oh well.

⤜ξ 23 ξ⤛

NO UMBRELLA

Did you ever walk down a city street on a rainy day—perhaps at the noon hour when everybody was out for lunch? Amazing, isn't it, the way the umbrellas bloom like big flowers of all kinds, taking the brunt of the wetness while the owners stay snug and dry underneath them.

An umbrella is a pretty handy thing to have around the house. You just never know when a storm will brew, and if you ventured out without it you'd find yourself soaked to the skin.

It seldom rained in California the years we lived there when our son was growing up. When it did, he turned very excited. He would race to his grandmother's closet, drag out her plaid umbrella, run out the door, put it up, and stride up and down all the streets around us, singing at the top of his lungs.

Once the brief storm was over, he'd shake the umbrella off and let it dry on the back porch. He'd forget it, usually, so that my mother or I had to bring it back into the house and put it in her closet again. Where it remained for all the very long times between rains.

Up in Oregon, a beautiful state in the summer, it rains almost every day and almost all day, during the winter. Umbrellas in Oregon seldom have a chance to dry out through those months. They're used all the time and are as important a piece of apparel as raincoats and boots.

I got to thinking the other day that most people seem to consider God an umbrella. They bring him out and ask him to cover and protect them only when the weather of their inner world is stormy. They forget him on the porch or put him away in the closet, like our son did his grandmother's (what did she call it?) "bumbershoot," when the atmosphere of their lives is clear and fresh.

I used to be that way. I cried, "God, God, God," in desperation. And when the desperation eased off, I stood on my own two feet and didn't ask him for any favors. I even felt proud because I didn't need to beg.

Not any more.

God is *not* an umbrella. But if he is to be used as one, it should be like the citizens of Oregon, who keep an umbrella handy at all times and use it every day. It just isn't fair to the Lord to keep him waiting somewhere in the wings of our lives, waiting for the moment when the lightning hits, the thunder roars, the rain pours down. When we need help, or strength, or courage.

It seems to me that God is not there to *protect* us from anything, anyhow. Not there just to reach down a beneficent hand and give us what we want. As a matter of fact, there's an old truism that says, "God help us all if we get what we ask for."

No, as we grow in faith, as we reach out to enhance the person we were born to be, God changes proportion in our minds, doesn't he? He becomes, if we strive hard enough, a daily Friend, not to be dragged into the picture just in times of stress, but to be communicated with, to be trusted. No Santa Claus with a bag of gifts we coax for. But someone wiser, deeper, broader, more everlasting, more knowing than we.

The way we pray is not so important as the consistency of our prayers. So that our minds are never free of God, and back inside of them is the constant knowledge of him.

I myself have simplified the whole process. I say many times every day, "God, please. God, thank you."

He knows what I need. He knows what I'm grateful for. And, I believe, he has no intention whatever of sheltering me from any pain, any trial, any misery. Instead, he feeds me in small part with his wisdom and his depth and his breadth —and that is enough.

47

✍ 24 ☙

THE DAISY FIELD

When I was young there was a daisy field across the street. It ran for three blocks long and almost as many wide. In certain seasons of the year we used to live in those daisy fields.

Once inside there was a new world—a world made up of the yellow centered flowers and their surrounding leaves, which stood as high as our heads. We could crumple down a hundred of them and make a room. Or push them into paths of a maze. We could string them together into crowns and bracelets and necklaces. We could live a thousand lives in half a day, thick in the daisy field.

When the whistle came from a homecoming father, or the high call from a mother, we would return, reluctantly, to the real world, always knowing that this other one was waiting and would hold for us as long as the daisies bloomed in the sun.

For today's children, the daisy field doesn't bloom in the sun. They are not safe alone on any street, in any park, in any field. And the private, long, dreaming day, un-supervised, is lost in the past. When you face a group of today's children, your own youth seems part of a gone dream. Where in these solid little citizens is your childhood? How do you bring it out, the best of the magic world that you lived in back there?

Today's children, too, live in the practical world of the spectator. They watch. TV. Outer space. Movies. Plays. Sports. Even the magical miracle of Disneyland translates into reality that which they should paint for themselves from words they read by themselves.

Too often, then, they do not know how to dream, or if they can, they do not see themselves as individual and apart, each filled with special inner treasure to be tapped and brought to the surface.

For a very long time, as a sort of extra hobby interest, I held classes in creative drama for children. To discover their specialness they each tried to remember back as far as they could. To stretch their imaginations they acted out fairy stories, given no words to say, no actions to make, except the wonderful inspirations that came to them on the spur of the moment. To learn to share they told each meeting the greatest and most exciting thing that had happened to them, and the whole class acted it out. To learn to feel for other people they walked old and young, and they crawled and cried and laughed and were clowns. They were everybody. And more, much more.

If I were a wealthy woman I would open such classes clear across the country, in every city and town where there were young ones. As I'm not, I can only tell about it. And I can hope too. I can hope that somewhere out there, you young parents, you'll hear and understand this youthful need for expression and self-investigation. That you may, perhaps, get together such a project in your own community. Or perhaps, and best of all, just not be too busy yourself to try it with your own youngsters and those in your neighborhood. Play it by ear. Make up all sorts of situations and memories. Take the time, time, time. You know what? There will be no communication difficulties later. Promise!

Children just cannot rise to your level at all times. Nor should they be shunted off with their contemporaries at all times. They need both.

Because—given the sense of being special, individual, aware of the breadth of the mind and imagination; able to communicate and share with those around them; able to speak clearly, to express ideas neatly, above all to dream—today's children will have a chance. A chance in a world of explosive tensions to gather a few daisies and make them into a chain that can sustain them when grown.

Because the daisy field is there all right. Latent—to be hunted out, planted, watered, and tended a little—but there. And it is our job to make it bloom in the sun as it once did for us.

◄§ 25 §►

INSTRUMENT OF GOD

Have you ever watched the television quiz shows? A woman stands or sits, nervously, before the microphone. Then, the master of ceremonies almost always asks· her the same question.

"And what is *your* occupation?"

The woman swallows twice, takes a deep breath, and says apologetically, "I'm just a housewife!"

Yes, you are a housewife. You are a woman. Because you are, the size of your world seems pretty small and petty sometimes. The daily round of housework, child care, taxi service, clubs, church, narrows your life and takes away some of its value.

Yet, because you are a woman, even because you are a housewife, you can get closer to greatness than most men can.

You have a piece of dirt outside your kitchen door. It's near the boxes where you put trash. It just sits there—a square of dust in the summertime, of mud in the spring, of hard clay in the winter.

One day you go to the store. There's a bonus sale at the counter beside the vegetables. Eighteen bulbs for thirty-nine cents. You pay for your groceries. By some small trick you

50

have thirty-nine cents left. On impulse you go back and pick up the string bag of bulbs.

When you have a free moment you take them out to that square. You dig little holes, maybe with an old fork because you don't have the right tools. You fix little puddles of water in each hole. And you set the bulbs carefully inside, packing the loose earth gently around each one. Then you water the whole thing and go back to whatever you have to do.

You feel strangely pleased, as if something had begun. Then you get busy and you almost forget. Until the morning when you walk into the kitchen and peek out to see what kind of a day it is.

And there they are! Green shoots. New green. A different green from any other grown green. Fresh, young, somehow questing.

The other day comes, too. The day when the jonquils—or the daffodils, the hyacinths, or the tulips—raise their chins to the sun—each one exquisitely marked, brilliant with color, perfectly shaped.

Then you stand and look at them. And you are filled with wonder. You don't put a name to the wonder, maybe. Maybe you only say to your husband or your oldest child, "Whaddyaknow. Spring is here. The daffodils are up."

But there *is* a name for the wonder. You think planting a bulb and helping a flower to grow isn't stretching the world wider? You think it isn't working with God?

What if he hadn't given you the thought to dig those holes and pour that water?

What if he hadn't made you, as he did, the instrument through which he could perform his miracles of growth?

Is that "just a housewife"? Is that a small thing?

⊷§ 26 §⊶

LETTER

I got a letter from my friend Eloise the other day.

"Joe has retired, as you know," she wrote, "and I'm ready to climb the walls. I don't know what to do about him. He follows me all over the house. Gets under my feet in the kitchen. Tries to tell me how to poach eggs. Sighs and moans, like the kids did when they used to come at me with the question, 'What can I do now?' What *can I* do?"

I didn't answer her, that part of the letter anyhow, because she probably wouldn't have paid any attention, and also because I felt so sorry for her.

Climb the walls, indeed!

I remember when the baby woke us up at the crack of dawn, or the alarm clock startled us from a happy dream and our feet hit the cold floor before we were conscious. All those years, those fast-moving, hard-working years.

Money can't buy the feeling, now, way back in my conditioned mind that it's past seven o'clock, and my husband has crawled out from his bed to mine and throws one arm around me with no demands, except to be warm and snug with me and doze until nine o'clock—or more.

Money can't buy the whole quiet house at night, and the books to read together, and maybe going downstairs together and having crackers and milk—the reading and the snacking geared to just as late an hour as we wish. And to know that when you *do* go to sleep, it will be deep and peaceful, because you don't have to worry about what time the kids will roll in and where they are and what they're doing.

Or in the morning when we wake up and there it is, a crystal fall day, and the October leaves are every shade in the world, and we can turn to each other and say, "Let's go to the state park and see the pillows of the hills and look at the reflections of the colors on the broad dam and have a hamburger at McDonald's." To be able to *do* it, with no thought of an office to get to, or work of any kind which *must* be done for an extra nickel, or kids to take to school and lessons of varying kind. Just to be *able* to do it, to live a day the way you want to live it, as it comes along.

It's a pleasure, too, on the practical side, to have a man along for your daily duties. Grocery shopping is a lot more fun if you consult each other, counting out not only the pennies, but the sort of food you'd like to share during the coming week. As for the food itself, it tastes better if you cook it when you both feel hungry, and eat it all over the house—on trays before the TV news, on the back porch on a soft day, in the kitchen where serving is easy. And if my semiretired husband wants to poach the eggs, I let him. He makes them better than I ever could. And he's improved on some of my tried and true recipes, too. Never mind the mess left over. There are now *two* of you to clean up.

After the busy years it's a joy to have your own older friends for dinner and not have to rush around getting the kids fed first and out of the way. It's nice to go to church, the two of you, when you *feel* like it, with no obligation for perfect attendance scores for the young in Sunday School. And it's equally interesting to sluff around in your pajamas and robe and take all Sunday morning to read the paper, to drink coffee and eat sausage and French toast, if you don't feel like church.

I'd like to tell Eloise that retired husbands and wives don't have to be together *all* the time. He has his luncheon clubs, his bowling nights, maybe even his golf. She has her bridge, discussion, and knitting groups. And off they go, each on his or her own way, to come back to each other refreshed and with bits of news.

Most importantly though, I'd like to say how exciting it is to try to get back into each other's minds. This is not the young man you married or just the father of your children. It's a discovery, after all the interrupted years, of that inner life of both of you separately, which has been growing and swelling and just waiting to be born—and shared. Sort of "How do you do, Mr. Smith. How are YOU?" After a lifetime of "Johnny has a cold" and "Susie is a problem."

One of the things said of two people in wedlock is that marriage is for two. I'm not always sure about that. But when a man gets that gold watch and moves on home to stay, I know for certain that the "golden years" can be just that—and also with certitude that retirement is for two!

Go climb your walls, Eloise.

27

THE TROUBLE WITH HATE

I have reached a stage where all I ask of any human being is that he keep his claws sheathed. When I do not ask anyone to do anything *for* me—but only that he does nothing *against* me. In short, that he does not hate.

Hate. Divide those whom life has touched unkindly, which is most of us at one time or another. It always comes out that there are those who, hurt badly, emerge as haters. And there are, in fewer number, those who manage to stay lovers after love has been crucified.

It is no simple thing to keep on loving—anybody, everybody, anything, everything—when the echoes of pain and injustice are still ringing in your ears.

The trouble with hate is that it was created by intense hurt from a specific source. Seldom is one able to battle this source successfully, in return, directly. More often, the defeat is total because hurt must always come to us from our weakest weakness—and usually from the person who has made us vulnerable—the one we love.

Shattered then, and stumbling inside like a wounded animal, unable to repay pain for pain, the hate builds up until we are nauseated with it and its rancid lump threatens to choke us. In bitterness, unable to tolerate the sight of those who apparently have not known similar pain, we lash out.

Sometimes this is done in great bold gestures, an angry book or play, a denial of all life, a murder or an assassination, a suicide. More often, though, the hate leaks out in small doses, almost always unexpectedly and in between normal kindnesses. And always against those who, in turn and as we once were, are vulnerable because they still love, still care.

This slow leakage does more damage because there is never a decisive battle but always a sort of cold war. It eats up years of contentment, takes the edge off any planned joy, and stretches the lovers taut and tense, trying to live as they believe, swallowing down the retort, searching for hidden good qualities.

As it is for one of us, so it is for the world.

There is so much hate, large sprawling clouds of it. Yet, it seems to me that all of it is based on the close simplicity of a personal harm done unjustly.

It has been a long time, looking from my personal life outward, since I have heard a kind and generous word, one human voice to another. There are still those heroic gestures, flung out in times of great stress. But they become as straightforward as the old idea that if one must die one should die well. It is the living who concern us, and just as hate leaks those small doses over a lifetime from a single hurt and damaged person, so has it seeped everywhere from a hurt and damaged world.

For many years now mankind, like the individual who turns his hurt to hate, has concentrated on the creation of the instruments of hate, the stockpiles of destruction. Like the individual, mankind has his choice. He may make hate's boldest gesture and blow up his world. He may let hate leak over generations in the scattered smaller murders in varied locations, the little wars, which we have lived with for a long time now.

Or he may turn his wounds to healing and love again. Again? Did he ever really love? Did he ever truly try?

This improbable choice is a solution mankind may never know. It's certain he will never know it until it is reduced to the lowest common denominator—of the kind word, the decent thought, the will not to harm because one has been hurt and feels the need to strike out.

You and I, believe it or not, are part and parcel of mankind. Could we maybe start a movement? Could we maybe, now, this minute, stop hating anything? Anybody? And give the power of love a little chance? I wonder.

⤳ 28 ⤲

THE EMPTY NEST

I walked out into the yard the other morning and stopped short under the evergreen elm. Lying in its shade, blown free by the wind, was a small empty nest. It was an intricate and delicate piece of architecture, threaded through with the cotton padding of our old chair on the back porch.

I stared down at the nest and remembered that just a few months ago two small quick birds had dared the shelter of that porch hundreds of times. A sudden swoop, a flashing snap, a right-about, and they had headed for the tree, soft white fluff in their beaks from our old stuffed chair. Over and over again.

The nest was finished when they no longer attacked that chair. The nest was filled when they made ravished darts upon the dry bread I left on the grass. The nest was sanctuary when three small uncertain birds were taught to leave it and return.

Now the nest was empty. The little ones were flying free. And where were the two who had worried and worked so long and hard to create, harbor, and feed them?

I looked around. Our house never seemed so big. So empty. So clean. All of them gone—our small birds, too.

And where were we two? We parent birds?

Oh, we'd been together, yes. But always as *parents*. Slowly, hardly noticing, we had lost our own names. We had become Mother and Father, or Mom and Dad. For years we lived vicariously, through the youth in our house. We gloried in victories, suffered over disillusions, shivered with dangers and illnesses. And now, that youth was gone from the nest.

Well, what's so bad about that?

Those two birds, gone from the evergreen elm, are flying somewhere together in a clear blue sky. They are together in the special way they were before they decided upon that tree and robbed our chair of its cotton.

That which was last is becoming first again. Two are wed—birds or people—after all, and may we live a long time, please, to appreciate the fact.

I picked the empty nest up carefully. It held together as firm as adobe, built to last. I took it to the garage and put it in a box, to keep it, to remind me.

Then I went back into the house and dug out that old recipe for a very complicated date torte, which had helped me win my husband in the first place. And which I really hadn't made, or even tried to, since the first baby was born.

57

I hoped that he would know how I felt about him when I served it to him, and I hoped, sincerely, that I still had the knack of making it. For him. For Don. For the man I married, not Daddy.

·ᴥᴥ 29 ᴥᴥ
THE OLD COOKBOOK

You know, if I were ever to write a cookbook—and now that I think of it, someday I may do just that—I'd call it *The My Mother Wrote it Down Cookbook*.

My mother wrote down some dandy recipes. But it's not for that alone that I would do her cookbook. Nor even because each time I read one of them I remember her, because the recipes are written in her handwriting, still young and firm although she is long since old and gone. No, it's that with each one of them I remember the person, the aura, the place where, as a child, I ate that special dish.

There was my aunt's house. It wrapped warm and soft and good smelling about me. My aunt sat before the fire. Around her were a cousin or two, a neighbor, a friend, somebody from the church, all with busy hands and flashing needles.

My aunt would get up finally, moving gently, and would bring the tea, allowing me to pass the cookies. The soft easy voices talked of all sorts of things, some of which I was banished from hearing.

But I loved to go there. I learned to featherstitch there. I learned to sit quietly, stare at the flames in the fireplace, and listen and relax.

When I see the recipe for those cookies—Sour Milk Drop Cookies—in my mother's writing, I am back there. I feel good, young and happy and safe.

I see across the page Aunt Nettie's Grape Pie. Aunt Nettie was my mother's aunt. I am moved back in time to that pie with its crust as rich as shortbread and the tart-sweet narrow filling of deep purple.

Aunt Nettie and Uncle Bert lived in a house that was dull and little and gray, where the trolleys racketed back and forth in echoing clangs on the street in front of it. But in the side parlor there was an upright piano. Everybody sang there. Grandpa had a beautiful untrained voice, and so did Uncle Charlie and Aunt Nettie's three girls. No matter how bad yours was, you couldn't do a thing to spoil the sounds they made.

Aunt Nettie had, too, a long narrow trestle of a dining-room table, which must have been especially made to hold as many as it did, ranked like starving soldiers, tight-squeezed on either side.

But it was the backyard that held me and my dreams, those long ago years. There was the arbor, and it seemed to go for miles, like a tunnel, with so little light pushing through the tightly woven vines that the world turned purply green.

There were the benches along the sides, and there I sat hour upon hour, listening to the music from the side parlor, squinting to make the sunbeams more spangly, breathing as deeply as I could to get somewhere inside of me the rich, pungent aroma of those thousand thousand grapes.

Aunt Nettie's Grape Pie, and I think of her, a bustler and an accomplisher and a superb cook. Then I rest awhile in the grape arbor. Strange and wonderful.

Oh, the recipes. Well, if you'd like them, here they are.

My Aunt's Sour Milk Drop Cookies
1½ cups sugar
½ cup shortening
2 eggs
4 cups flour

Little salt and nutmeg
Vanilla
2 teaspoons baking powder in flour
1 level teaspoon soda in sour milk
1 cup sour milk
Mix all together. Drop from teaspoon closely on greased cookie sheet. Hot oven.

Aunt Nettie's Grape Pie

Wash and seed 3½ cups of purple grapes. Stir into them 1½ to 2½ tablespoons quick tapioca and 1 to 1½ cups of sugar. The leeway is whether you want thick or thinner, tart or sweeter.

Let mixture stand for about 15 minutes and put it into an unbaked pie shell. Bake at 450° F. for 15 minutes, then turn back to 350° for 20 to 30 minutes more.

With the first bites, you'll be in my aunt's house before the fire or in the grape arbor yourself. I promise!

⋞ 30 ⋟

GIFT WITHOUT THE GIVER

I expect all of us like to think of ourselves as both kind and generous, don't we? We give where we can to all sorts of things, bake cakes for ill neighbors, or work hard on worthwhile projects. But, *how* are we generous?

Once in my life there was a wonderful woman whom I loved. She did much for me, and to this day I am grateful. But still, one little episode stays in my mind.

We were shopping together in a very fine store. On a rack there were simple but quite handsome dresses reduced to eight dollars. I was in college, the depression was not yet over, and I knew the upcoming year would be hard for my father to manage.

The woman I loved called me over to the hat counter and showed me a beautiful piece of headgear, a picture hat of rough straw with taffeta crown and a flat bow in just the right place.

"Try it on," she said. I did. I was young, I was tanned and healthy and smooth skinned. I really looked pretty great.

"Would you like this hat?" she asked me.

I stared at myself and then my eyes moved to the rack of reduced dresses. "How much is the hat?" I asked her.

"Thirty-five dollars," she said, sounding proud somehow.

I did some rapid arithmetic. Four times eight made thirty-two. "I need dresses badly," I explained. "We could get *four* of those for thirty-two."

She pulled herself tall. "You may," she announced, "have the hat or nothing at all." I took it—in a hurry. I had it for years and loved it and still loved her. But I've never forgotten.

I knew a man once who was very generous too. He would give his considerable bounty by the handful. But if you wanted to, or were forced to, take of that bounty, you had to do it in *his* way. You had to go to the school he chose. Or buy the suit he liked on you. Or accept the luxury gift when you needed necessities. He imposed himself before the gift. The strings attached very often made the gift itself meaningless and petty.

I knew a woman once who spent much of her life helping other people. She went miles around when neighbors were ill, her basket over her arm, her big apron wrapped around her.

She took over. Until the new mother was able to be up. Until the weak old woman regained her strength. The broken arm healed. The frayed nerves mended. These times this good woman would run the house.

All the same, people didn't like to see her coming. Because once they were on their feet again, it took a lot of work to get their surroundings back to normal. This good woman literally took over. She cleaned as if the house hadn't been cleaned in ten years. She cooked new foods as if all the old family recipes were unhealthy. She moved furniture and changed schedules.

Being human, she didn't keep still about it. She told others how much she had improved everything. And her criticisms were a reflection, of course, on the normal routine and arrangement, the family's usual way of life.

Once more a gift was nullified by the imposition of its donor's personality.

Certainly it's not an easy thing to submerge yourself when you are being a giver. But equally certain, it's mighty important to try to do so. The whole basic premise of giving anybody anything, even a Christmas or birthday gift, is to *please* them. To make them happy. And who can be happy with a gift that implies the receiver is a dunce, or a beggar, or incompetent to handle what they receive?

Goodness knows, I don't have much to give, materially at least. But the next time I give a kid so much as a penny, I'm not going to tell him how to spend it. And the next time I give of myself, nobody is going to know it except the person I try to share myself with—and *no* advice goes with it!

⋙ 31 ⋘

HALF EMPTY? HALF FULL?

Once upon a time, there were two prospectors in the middle of the Mojave desert in July. They came down out of the rock hills in their old car. The miles shimmered ahead of them, alive with heat.

They bumped along the unpaved road that led to the highway, looking forward to the town ten miles away and the small cafe, which served hot dinners and cold drinks and was air-cooled.

The old car stopped. It stopped dead and suddenly and for no reason. They worked on it. For a long time they worked, until they were weak and soaked to their skins and avoiding each other's eyes.

One of them said, "We'll have to walk it. Nobody ever comes up this old road."

The other nodded. He went back to the car and brought out a clear bottle. It showed a water line neatly in the middle.

He held it up for a terrible, silent moment and licked his lips. "We'll never make it," he said weakly. "It's ten long miles. And the bottle is half empty."

The other one forced a smile.

"Sure we will," he insisted. "It's only ten miles—and the bottle's not half empty. It's half full. Let's go."

I hate to leave you there. As a matter of fact, I hate to leave the two men there. I don't know whether they made it or not. But I'm pretty sure, if either one of them made it, which one it was.

My mother and her best friend were "callers" for the church they attended. It kept them busy and active. More, it kept them feeling young. My mother and her friend, as a matter of fact, are worthy of a thought, a nod, a pat. Having lost their lives, they and so many others when they lost their husbands, they found new lives. Quite simply and with no dramatics, they discovered all sorts of small things with which to fill their diminishing years. And they discovered a few big things. Being "callers" was one of those. When they went out to make their visits, they went into another world, into the world of the truly old, the amazingly ancient.

Sometimes, when they came back from the rest homes or the private homes or the hospitals, they were silent and depressed, and it took a while for them to get back on an even keel.

Other times they almost sprinted into the house, full of a story about a ninety-three-year-old sparking gallantry or an eighty-six-year-old who told them a funny story. Some of their "old people" they loved and looked forward to seeing. Others they felt very sorry for, and they tried not to drag their heels when they had to go to see them.

Listening to their talk I thought I found the difference between their two kinds of ancients. One set wore the years with grace—wearing a thin, lacelike cloak like exquisite hand tatting. It contained nany silken threads, enough to make it shine. And they had created it of remembrance, vague sometimes, filmily recalled through dim eyes, the slow-moving heart, the slightly confused mind. They had created it of many things. Tenderness, adventure, gaiety, innocence, marriage, understanding, tolerance, responsibility, patience, compromise, balance, authority, self-control—and the defeat of defeat. They had left behind the memory of sand and storm and dark thread. They had distilled and purified and looked ahead into serenity.

And the others? The ones whom my mother and her friend, no matter how great their pity, were reluctant to visit?

They were the ones who had lived it all, too, but had not allowed themselves to look inward. They were the ones whom no life, however overlong, had been able to teach. Unadjusted, struggling, regretting, everything still unfound, they wore a clumsy, coarse, and ill-fitting cloak. They still tasted the grit and the sting, and the dust stayed in their eyes, and it would stay until they stopped breathing.

At that time, at the last breath, they would depart like one of our men in the desert, feeling that the bottle of their life had always been half empty. The others, the trying and hopeful who left life knowing the bottle was half full, as they had known it always, may easily find a joyful surprise in store for them.

They may find that it was a very full vessel, indeed.

<del>≈§</del> 32 <del>§≈</del>

HEAD OF THE HOUSE

When I was little, a long time ago, I used to sit on his lap and listen to grandfather tell poems—long, sad, dramatic ones—and hum soft, sentimental old songs.

My grandfather worked in a factory. He brought the smell of it in with him, a sort of steel tartness that I found pleasant. It was on his clothes and on his hands and in his pores, even when he was freshly washed and dressed. I used to lean against him and sniff the strange odor. In my mind I could hear, through the humming, the noises of the plant.

My grandfather's head was as bald as an egg, with a perfect semicircle of gray ruffled hair around it. He had a moustache, which matched that sprouting hair, and he had very blue eyes. He wore gray sweater coats, the kind that button down the front, and he had a fat gold watch, which he pushed with his thumb to make the lid spring up and the face with its bold black numbers spring out.

When my grandfather came home, everything in the simple flat where he lived began to hum, too. The hot water in the teakettle seemed to wait for his step to shoot up its geyser. The salt-rising bread in the oven seemed to time itself to reach a golden brown just as he dried his hands. The creamed salt pork began to thicken. The potatoes almost mashed themselves. The green beans, which had stayed hard all afternoon over the low fire, suddenly were tender and crunchy. The two-crust lemon pie was pricked out with his initial—a big W oozing sugary yellow.

My grandfather never had much money in the little tan envelope spread out on the kitchen table after Saturday night's supper was finished. But all of his family was there to watch the proceedings and to receive, if they merited it in his eyes, a speck of the change from the weekly portion.

It was a good and proud moment in the kitchen of the old flat. When it was over, and grandma had received her house money, and the various little tobacco cans with their labels for monthly bills had taken their share, my grandfather jingled what was left in his hand. He gave it a high jingle that shot the money up into the air and back, spinning and silver and looking like more than it was.

Then he put on his sweater coat and his cap. He patted everybody on the head, bent to tickle the neck of the youngest with his moustache, and walked out of the door.

He sauntered down the street to the newspaper and confectionery store. He bought himself two tins of tobacco to last the week through and a hometown paper. He never got used to the fat city dailies. He talked to his cronies and wandered back home.

In his sweater pocket, the one which didn't hold the tobacco, was a striped bag of rock candy for my grandmother. This she accepted, when he settled down in the rocker across from her, with as much delight as if it were a five-pound box of chocolates with a big pink bow, and with as much surprise as if he didn't buy her an identical bag every Saturday.

Grandpa was the head of the house. How few, how very few of them there are nowadays. But, a passing thought, wouldn't it be worth a loving woman's trouble to try to make her husband feel that way—now—today?

P.S. My grandmother's teeth weren't very good. Rock candy set them on edge. But every Saturday night she emptied that little bag.

P.P.S. Here is my grandmother's recipe for Two-Crust

Lemon Pie. You just dot in the initial with a regular kitchen fork—BIG!

Take 2 scant cups of flour and a teaspoon of salt. Sift over ⅔ cup of shortening and cut in well. Add 4 tablespoons of water, one at a time, and mix light but well with a fork. Roll gently (a light hand for crust always), add filling and top crust, and bake in moderate 350° F. oven till golden brown. Oh, yes, the filling. It's just 1½ level cups sugar; 2 large eggs, beaten; juice of 1½ lemons, stirred till creamy.

❦ 33 ❧

THE GOLDEN YEARS?

The other night, with a group of old friends, we got to talking about what it meant to be fifty years old—or older, as most of us were. We decided that it would be an experiment almost worth the trying to make a book of all the people who have walked through our lives, gallantly, with half a hundred years written on their faces and in their gaits. Different. All so different.

It would be nice if attaining that age would, or could, mean we were settled and sure, and things had quieted down a little and would stay that way.

But they don't. You've seen it, as I have.

Maybe that's what we get for beginning to be reconciled to life, for saying to ourselves, "Well, I had it tough and fought it through, and I deserve this comfortable middle-aged lull and I'm going to enjoy it."

Crazy life. Never, or almost never, do we relax our vigilence and loosen our grip and trust the whole process completely, but out of the blue comes a hand to upset the apple cart. Many times it comes in the fifties, or even later.

Sometimes it seems as if life is a series of boxes neatly tied with ambitions or hopes or despair and stored in the attic of the mind, dusty with neglect, but there, each separate and distinct from its fellow. Babyhood, kindergarten, school, high school, college, the first job, courtship, marriage, parenthood, grandparenthood. Anybody who is fifty or over has packed away those universalities. As for the world around us, anybody who is sixty remembers World War I, the Roaring Twenties, Black Friday, the depression, World War II, the years of truce, Korea, the cold war, Vietnam—and this very moment's confusion and chaos.

How have the fifties and over coped with it all? Wouldn't it be nice if the young people would ask us once in a while?

They had—and have—*courage*. It came in small doses, probably. It wasn't always tested to its tautest, thinnest tone. But day after day, week in and week out, month's end and year's end, life showed what it had to offer. It nibbled or snapped, and sometimes it gouged. It hurt. But each time it was managed. Time added to time, small bravery added to bravery. Finally there was enough, given enough time, given enough living, enough survival.

Fifty has lived. Fifty has survived. It's very nice at this age if some dreams have come true, some practical dreams. It's good to have finished paying for the roof over your head, to see your way clear to retiring in fair comfort later, to know the kids have good educations and started good jobs, even made you a baby-sitter again.

But once more, as in all ages, these are not the greatest, deeper satisfactions that bring sound sleep and good taste in the mouth. What does, instead, is the fact that at fifty or more you have picked up your load. You have carried it strongly. You have a reserve on which to draw, all that you have lived and thought and felt. You have *resources!* You are realistic. You have no false pride any more. You know, most importantly, what counts in the long run and what doesn't. What money can buy and what it can't. You know that half a loaf may not nourish for as long as a whole one, but it is equally sustaining while it lasts.

These are the ingredients that, put together, make up a big shelf of courage. This is what is meant by that too-slick phrase "emotional maturity." It is a phrase that is not to be won in a moment or a decade or in three or four. It takes a while. It takes the whole time of your life, the whole time of living.

Emotional maturity is like having glasses made for you that are no longer so finely ground for distance that you cannot see what is right before you in your own hands. Instead, they are glasses that clarify and enlarge and sharpen your vision wherever you look. And they protect you from any sudden gusts of dust.

Well, that's the conclusion my friends and I came to the other evening. And when we did (you know something?) we didn't feel badly at all about growing older, or even old.

⊷ 34 ⊶

UNCLE ART

Where we live there is a peninsula that rides out into the lake. The other day, in the snow, we took a ride out there. To see how it looked in the wintertime. To find out if it had been further eroded. To watch whatever wildlife there was.

It brought back so many memories that they crowded my mind. But most of all, it brought back Uncle Art.

In the old days the peninsula was a crooked index finger extending from the palm of the hand of land. It beckoned in a deep green angle across the bay to the public dock, still so much the same now, at the foot of State Street.

In those days, when my Uncle Art was young, only the matching dock and small clearing on the opposite edge of the cup of water were civilized. The rest of it was a temperate-zone jungle, with paths marked only by adventurers into the darkness, covered over and over again by Joe the Hermit, who disliked all roads and human tracks and most people.

The first thing Art ever owned, aside from his books, was the canoe he bought from one of the few remaining Indians around the fort at Niagara Falls. It was well and handsomely made, with hand decorations he learned to decipher. He saved through his sixteenth to eighteenth year to pay for it. And it set him free the moment he lifted it, light and waterworthy, atop his shoulder and strode all the way down State Street, as if he were portaging it from stream to stream through wild Canadian territory.

It set him free, and it gave him his girl alone. Nobody could reach them, paddling so quietly with only the silver whispered sounds of three drops of water from their oars, or could touch them, lost together on the water or in the depth of the peninsula.

Saturdays, Sundays, evenings after working in a factory, he and Katrine would move together to the public dock, load the small craft with their books to read, their sandwiches and bottles of water and milk, and they would shove off into the quiet. They were beautiful people, especially to me, a child of seven then.

Our backyard, in the darkest, shadiest places, bloomed a garden different from any other in the neighborhood, or in town for that matter. Strange lacy ferns leaned protectively over all the shy flowers—the anemones and violets and smallest Johnny-jump-ups. There was no wire around them, but Art, by telling all us children what they were, where he found them, how they grew, instilled a "don't touch" that never failed.

Art and his girl didn't find Joe the Hermit. He found them. And he liked them, their entity, the almost-silence that

70

matched the silent world, the blending with earth and trees—things which Joe the Hermit recognized and welcomed. Whatever, he shared himself and his rough cottage with them, entrusted his staple shopping to them, respected their aloneness, but opened his door whenever they were ready for him.

It was a good world, there on the old peninsula before the state road was put through, before the bathing houses were built, and the men and women, the turnouts and the police barracks, the numbered swimming beaches and the state-owned barbecues, litter baskets and free stacks of wood. It was a secret waiting for those who could appreciate it and had the courage to face the snakes and insects and who knows what wild animals that could, and probably did, inhabit it. It was Art's world and his girl's, and it could have led to a life unlike any other, quite.

But it didn't, of course. The peninsula changed. The whole world changed. And Art died of a ruptured appendix three months before he would have been twenty-one.

What tricks the memory of childhood plays, though. Riding with the heaped up snow beside us, on a wide good road smooth beneath us, I had the strange feeling that if I turned my head quickly, it would be summer long ago. They would be there, leaning against a rough tree, with one bird above them breaking his heart in song.

᷈৩ 35 ৡ᷈

THE SWANS AND THE GOOSE

Where we came from, the eastern shore of Maryland, the gentle waters run in and out like fingers, curl into smaller creeks and coves like tender palms. The Canada geese know this, as do the fat white swans and the ducks who ride an inch above the waves of Chesapeake Bay. They come in by the thousands in the autumn.

In the hunting season the geese are fair game. It is different with the swans who are protected by law and who move toward the shores in a stately glide, lower their long necks deep in the water, and use their strong beaks to dig food from the bottom. There is between the arrogant swans and the prolific geese an indifference, almost a disdain. They have nothing to do with each other.

But this is a true story, which happened to a friend of mine. On one of the rare times when the river and the creeks were frozen over, she looked out of her huge window. Suddenly she leaned forward and peered. "It really is," she cried aloud. "There's a goose out there." Through her binoculars the figure of a large Canada goose, very still, his wings folded tight to his sides, his feet frozen to the ice, came clear. She worried. She went on the dock with a pole. It was too short. The ice was too thin to hold her weight, too heavy for the rowboat.

Then, from the dark sky she finally saw a line of swans. They moved in their singular formation, graceful and free. They crossed from the west high above the house toward the east.

As my friend watched, the leader swung to the right. Then the white string of birds became a white circle, floated from the top of the sky downward, and at last, as easy as feathers coming to earth, the circle landed on the ice.

My friend was afraid. Afraid that the goose might be pecked by those great swan bills. Instead, amazingly, those bills began to work on the ice as deliberately as picks swung over the head of a fisherman cutting free space for his rod. For a long time. Until at last the goose was rimmed by a narrow margin of ice. The swans rose again, following the leader, and hovered in that circle, awaiting the results.

The goose's head was lifted. His body pulled. Then the goose was free and standing on the ice, moving his webbed feet slowly. The swans stood in the air over him, watching.

As if he had cried, "I cannot fly," four of the swans came down around him. Their powerful beaks scraped the goose's wing from bottom to top, scuttled under his wings and rode up his body, chipping off and melting the ice held in the feathers.

Slowly, as if testing, the goose spread his wings as far as they would go, brought them together, spread again. When they at last reached their full, the four swans took off and joined the hovering group. They resumed their eastward journey in perfect impersonal formation to a secret destination.

Behind them, rising with incredible speed and joy, the goose moved into the sky. He followed them, flapping double time, until he caught up and joined the last of the line, like a small dark child at the end of a crack-the-whip of older boys.

My friend watched them until they disappeared over the tips of the farthest trees. Only then did she realize that tears were running down her cheeks and had been for how long she didn't know.

There are "bird people" who say this cannot happen. But they are wrong. It *did* happen. It's true. I do not try to interpret it. I just think of it in the bad moments, and from it comes only one hopeful question.

If so for birds, why not for man?

⋖§ 36 §⋗

WORRY IS A MOUSE

Awhile back we had a little visit together about fear. But I got to thinking the other night when I couldn't sleep, about the difference between fear and *worry*.

I thought, "Fear is a lion. Worry is a mouse."

There was a time (remember?) when you didn't know the meaning of worry. A time when you had to make up troubles to have something to feel dramatic about. Whether the hem of a party dress fell just right. Whether the boy you liked best would call you for that first date. Whether you'd pass with a decent grade, or if you'd pass at all.

Younger still, whether you'd be allowed to stay up an extra half hour on Friday night or would get to the circus when it came to town. You could cook up quite a storm about those things. As I did. As everybody did. But you weren't actually troubled. You had an underlying optimism, a wonderful quality most of us are born with, that things would work out to your advantage. Just because you were *you* and somehow special.

Well, as the years roll on we all know we're not special. The big crises come, and we are given extra strength to face them. The bullet hits all of us at one time or another, in one way or another, and somehow we have great, calm, sheer bravery to take it.

And after the crisis? After the situation ends? That's when worry begins. Faith, as we work for it with our living, is not only a matter of the heart, of emotion. It is a matter of the mind as well. Worry, too, is a matter of the mind. It must be dealt with, the habit broken, to leave any room for faith to grow. So let's try to deal with the little residue of worry that is left in some corner of our minds after its source has been removed. After the crisis. Like the nicotine that never quite gets out of a smoker's lungs. Or the hidden tartar that remains on our teeth even after the most careful brushing.

During the almost four years that my husband was in service in World War II, each morning with my first waking I lay still, eyes closed. Slowly, inevitably, a heaviness crawled through me, as if my blood were weighted with depression. The quietness of my night's sleep, its refreshment, was pushed away by that slow tide. When I pulled myself out of bed, I picked up my day with reluctant hands, no matter how busy I kept them or how bright the smile on my face. Did that happen to you?

Well, it was natural. Those were hard times. But here is what came next. When the war was over, my husband home, a baby born, there was still the half-waking, half-sleeping moment when the conditioning, the habit, of the war years took over. My mind, so accustomed to, so lost without, worry, scrabbled for new sources of sustenance. The baby's colic. The weight I should lose. The bills to be paid. The crack in the ceiling plaster.

It never, that mind of mine, I'm ashamed to say, stood still and proud and happy to count its morning blessings. Does this happen to you?

Worry is like a hangover must be. Waking in the morning, suddenly tense, with a mind jumbling and fussing, the world reeling, head pounding, trying to find something to grab, to hold to. And when the worrying mind finally latches on to a new little worry, there is almost relief, just to be busy with a familiar task.

So—worry is a habit. All right. We all worry, and what can we do to break the habit? Any habit, we are told by authorities on them, from alcoholism to a nervous giggle, can be broken. *If* the possessor of the habit has, first, a real desire to put a stop to it. *If* there is something else, something constructive to put in its place, to substitute. The world is filled with big problems. Not one of them is better solved by loss of sleep, by tied-up nerves, by the headaches and backaches and the shakes, that are the companions of worry.

So let's, right now, truly and sincerely, admit that we do not want to complicate our lives with the habit of worry. Then, let's begin to fight the blind emotion of worry with our minds. And with our belief in a *Power*—any power we choose. If that Power can create a brain, it can govern the brain it made, can keep it organized and neat and orderly. It can put worry where it belongs, like sweeping the kitchen floor until all the dust is in one corner. It can furnish the dustpan that will take worry off the floor of our brains entirely. And the ash heap on which to toss it. Then, we let it blow. Let the Power blow the worry wherever it wants to, while we enjoy our spic-and-span mind, our controlled thinking.

Then, when the scrabbling begins and the confusion, we say to *somebody*—"No dust in my house."

We have taken a big step in faith. We have made a clear spot on which faith can be rooted.

ᵂᵉᵍ 37 ᵍᵉᵂ

BEAUTY'S RIGHT

I watch more television than I should, which means I see more commercials than anybody should be subjected to. There are so many exquisite females caressing themselves, their hair, their hands, their slim legs. And I think about different forms of beauty.

I watch the young ones going to school, or in the stores, or loving themselves on TV, or modeling clothes, or enlarged beyond belief in a movie close-up. And I feel sorry for them.

I am sorry because they will someday be as old as I, yes. But I'm sorry for other reasons, too, I think, looking at them, of an old phrase from a very old Thomas Campion poem, "Give Beauty all her right. She's not to one form tied."

For years now I have seen beauty in many forms, looked for it, found it, on many unphotogenic faces.

When Jo Ellen was eighteen, they tell me, she was a very pretty girl. She is now past thirty and lives in a wheelchair. In the years between she has known the agony of twenty-six operations to repair the damage done in one blinding moment when the car in which she was riding collided head-on with another going at high speed.

People call on her, doing their good deed for the church or themselves. They walk into the cramped room, notice the twisted tiny body, the chiming gay bracelets next, the flower-splashed scarf that covers the head where the worst injuries remain, the bright lipstick on the mouth that is permanently nailed down at one corner. Eventually, when their shock and pity have subsided, they come to Jo Ellen's eyes and halt there and are held. They listen to Jo Ellen's laugh and the way her voice lifts and falls.

When they are once more at home, the realization comes that they have been in the presence of beauty. Jo Ellen stays in their minds, an afterglow that colors their days. Everybody else died in that collision. And Jo Ellen's love of the simple act of being alive is a form of beauty which they cannot forget. Courage, an earned loveliness.

In high school there was a gawky girl who kept much to herself, wore thick glasses, and was painfully shy. Except in Latin class. Called upon to translate a passage, she would pull herself awkwardly from the narrow seat and stand, hump-shouldered for the first line or so. Then, before our eyes she would grow tall and straight, and the phrases rolled easily from her lips until we could see how it was in those days of Rome. The beauty of intelligence.

77

There is a doctor I know, small, sandy, inconspicuous, with whom I shared a death. I tried to talk to the man in the coma, to tell him of his goodness. The doctor said, "He can't hear you. It's no use." And all the time, over and over, while his deft, dedicated hands were performing the services he knew were useless, his tender voice repeated, "It's all right, Dad. It's all right, Dad."

It could have been the film in my eyes, but a halo of beauty circled the simple little doctor. Around his face and in his eyes lived the grief for all the ones he had lost, those whose last sensation of touch was his, whose final rich comfort was the beauty of his compassion.

In our old neighborhood there was a little bug of a woman, eighty-five years old, bustling, bringing a parade of puddings, cookies, knitted slippers to her friends. She rang the bell three times and would come in on a wave of bright chatter and say, with no self-consciousness, "You are my friend," or "I just love you."

To save my life I couldn't tell you exactly what she looked like, but I can tell you what she felt like. She felt like that one described by Byron: "She walks in Beauty like the night."

In these strange and so often alienated times, it's good to look for such beauty. The loveliness of kindness, of faith, of sincerity, of hope, of courage, of joy, of humility. Because, you know, when you think about it, beauty that turns the head is as brief as a morning fog. Beauty that turns the heart lasts forever and grows as it ages.

What we put *on* our eyes does not count as much as what we put *in* them. It takes a lot of living to get that kind of makeup on right.

THE ORGANIZED FAMILY

Down the street and around the corner, in a city where we once lived, there was the best organized family I have ever seen. It consisted of a stocky, sturdy mother with busy eyes; a long, wiry father with fast feet; and three children, in high school, junior high, and elementary school.

They had the most expensive home on the block. The lawn was always neatly trimmed. The paint was perpetually fresh. Wall-to-wall carpeting inside, heavy custom-made drapes, a small grand piano. Television set. The biggest refrigerator, freezer, stove.

Sometimes I would sit on our front porch, shaking my head over our own summer-dried lawn, and watch them come and go. That is exactly what they did. They came. They went. They came back again. No two of them together. Always in movement. The mother would head down the street first, in the good car, zooming to her good job as a secretary for an insurance man. The high school boy wheeled by on his motorcycle next, headed for school. He never returned until after dark, after the supermarket where he worked was closed. The thirteen-year-old and the nine-year-old were next to whiz by me on carefully shined and oiled bicycles. They came home after school, pedaling hard. I knew what their hurry was. The teen-ager delivered our paper and all the others of a big route, and he had them all to fold, all those collections to make. The nine-year-old faced the tidying of the house and the starting of dinner. It was rumored he could peel a potato without the waste of a flake. In the middle of the afternoon the father, in a roaring jalopy, headed out for his job as night supervisor of a big plant. Sometimes, when I didn't sleep well, I could hear his returning roar well after midnight.

I was even known to reproach my own family about the integrated industry of the people down the street and around the corner. "They make lists," I said. "They have bulletin boards. Everybody has his job to do—and does it!"

I started to make a list once. I was interrupted and never got back to it. I did buy a bulletin board. It was filled, quickly, with blue ribbons for swimming, a picture of Wyatt Earp, a prayer for children, and pictures of pirates.

The reason I didn't follow through, I guess, is that I spent part of a Sunday afternoon in that nicest house. I did it by accident, because I didn't know the people. Nobody in our neighborhood did. You can't get acquainted with birds on the wing.

I saw it because the nine-year-old stopped by and asked to use our phone. Theirs was out of order. After I reported it for him, I offered him some cookies and milk. "Can't thanks," he clipped. "I have to get home. Ma's sick. Dad's at work. Sandy's at his job, Dick's baby-sitting——"

I insisted on going back with him. "I shouldn't take your time," he protested. The mother was really ill. I did what I could for her. "I hate to take your time," she said. "I just can't afford to be sick," she fretted.

Freddie stood in the doorway. "Time for homework," he stated. "Everything's been checked off." The mother said, "Remember this is the night for polishing all the shoes."

They were certainly organized! When I left the mother said, "You shouldn't have taken the time."

Before I let myself out I stood for a moment in the immaculate living room. It looked like a picture in a magazine. It looked as if nobody had used a chair or switched on the TV or opened a book. Matter of fact, there were no books.

Books take time. It looked, that living room, as if nobody lived in it. As nobody did.

On the way home I thought, "I bet they have money in the bank. I bet they're paying on a dozen installment purchases. I bet by the time they're forty they'll own the house, the father will be head of his department, the mother an executive-type, Sandy managing a supermarket at twenty-two, Dick a circulation man at eighteen and little Freddie working his way through college waiting on tables."

They were in their thirties, I guess—the important and doing years, making hay while the sun shines, the thrifty time. But when did they talk together? When did they think together, or alone? When did they ever even have time to sit down and enjoy looking at the material possessions for which they were all exchanging those unrecapturable hours of their lives?

That's when I threw away my bulletin board. And discarded all lists.

⋖§ 39 §⋗

BE A HAPPY LADY

You know, every once in a while, in a world of a lot of really nice and good people, you run into someone who is especially interesting. Especially so, perhaps, because he or she shares the ideas that you have not expressed but have thought time and again. This happened to me recently.

I met a young woman at a small gathering. We got to talking about children in a quiet corner together, and she came up with a story. It's not in her words, because I don't remember them exactly, but this is what happened to her.

She woke slowly one day, fumbling through the fog of exhaustion of having her first and, as yet, only child being about two years old. In the back room the singing lilted up and down, light as only a very young child's voice can be light, pure and sweet and without final cadence. Between the singing phrases there came a powerful change of tone. "Mommy, Mommy, Mommy."

She lay in the bed, and the darned sunshine was in her blinking eyes. Every worry in the world was in her littered mind. Her head ached, her corn hurt, and the coffee was yet to be made.

She stumbled from the bed and worked her way painfully into the back room. She didn't look directly at the uplifted, eager face.

She said, petulantly, "Why in the world do you have to wake up so early?"

"It's morning time." The little voice was suddenly slightly uncertain. "Boy's hungry."

She weaved out of the room. She shook her husband's shoulder. "Wake up, Daddy," she muttered. "Wake up." The little voice sang out again. "Wake up, wake up, wake up." Daddy didn't stir.

It broke inside of her, she told me, the sleeping, the fog, the corn, the headache, the tough day ahead. "For heaven's sake," she shook Daddy. "Wake up, darn you."

The singing in the back room stopped. There was silence for a moment, echoing her early morning tantrum. Then the little voice came clear, sure, with a note of authority. "Don't be a cross lady. Be a happy lady. Don't say darn. Say dear."

She said dear. She tried to say it nicely, even before she'd had her coffee. And she thought, "Me? Know it all? Know anything?"

She had been handed a lecture on living, in a high young voice, a voice with only a little over two years' experience in its vocabulary.

After that, she looked at her child in the morning and saw the happiness welling up into his face. She saw it foggily, perhaps, but she really saw it.

Watching him, she stared back down the years and remembered what it was like to wake up young. Why, the day was a gift package. It could be filled with anything. Good. Exciting. Wondrously new. The day was all mixed up with the blood that raced gaily through a rested small body and the sleep that was a cushion for the hours ahead. It was a day of golden sunshine, or a day of soft, gray rain, or a day of white snow. It didn't matter. It was a day. It was a thing of life offered by hands that were only sensed.

Consider this. Consider what our child can remind us of. The ignorance of tomorrow. It has been said in many ways before. But it is very easy to forget. Live today. This moment. This hour. Live, not with that wild huzzah for intemperance, "Eat, drink, and be merry for tomorrow we die." Not that way at all. But as a child lives, totally in joy, totally in sorrow, forgetting yesterday, with tomorrow a million miles away, with today stretching infinitely to a time when anything can happen.

The woman ended. "So now," she said, "I lie in bed one extra minute. I listen to the voice in the back room and let the small singing and the calling come to me and fill me and push away the worries and the meannesses. I look at the sleepy rosy face, its curved bright smile, and I put the echo of it on my own lips.

"I say, 'Good morning, dear. How are you this lovely day?'

"Do you know what he says? 'Happy boy. Happy Mommy.' Well, maybe not always the latter. But I'm trying," she told me. "I'm trying to follow his example, to learn, consciously, the joy that is his without thought."

And so can we. Can't we? Even if there is no small singing voice any longer in our nursery.

REAL WOMEN'S LIB

I got to thinking about men the other day. Now don't do any clucking of tongues about a woman as old as I doting on the opposite sex. Not a thing like that in the world. I swear! But with all the jockeying for position between the sexes nowadays, sometimes I have a queasy little feeling of pity for the males.

I heard a man say, in disgust, a few weeks ago: "Times sure have changed. My father used to bring home a pay envelope with real cash in it. Now money doesn't mean much. Some of us never see an amount in cash worth mentioning from year to year. It all happens by check, with the deductions already out, spoken for before it's received. There's never enough to go around anyhow. And what am I working so hard for?"

It's a good question and worth thinking about.

I believe that what any man is working so hard for is the expression on his children's faces when he gives them an allowance or a special treat, the expression of "Gee, Dad. For me?"

What any man is working so hard for is the look in his wife's eyes, the old-fashioned look that says: "You're a fine, big, strong man. You take good care of us. I don't know what we'd do without you."

When was the last time you saw children utterly enchanted by any gift? In words or looks and action? When was the last time you saw a man take a deep breath and stand a little taller because his wife said or did or looked a way that added a few inches to his stature?

The Bible talks about "whither thou goest" and following after. And in many ways, physical ones, women do. But there are other more subtle ways than moving from place to place as a man takes on a new job. The less tangible ways to follow. The most rewarding. The secret of this kind of "whither thou goest" seems to be lost in our time. The meaning of "follow" seems to elude today's woman. For the home, for the modern couple, this is a sorry, sad thing.

Women asked for it and they got it. Now they don't know what to do with it. Emancipation. Equality. Freedom. A place in the sun. Granted, they only wanted to walk arm in arm. Admitted, they just wanted to be partners side by side. But the whole thing, in our old-fashioned estimation, got out of hand.

Within the range of my acquaintance, I can count on the fingers of one hand the number of women who are truly happy. Now, why is this?

I believe it is because men today have to live against their true natures. They pulse with ulcers and heart attacks, because they are not meant to turn inward upon themselves, to swallow the retort to authority, to eat of themselves in silence. Yet, strangely, today's men have been forced to do just that. And they know a sense of loss. Loss of what? They don't know what. Sometimes, without this knowledge, but instinctively trying to compensate for the unadmitted loss, men drink too much, or become involved with other women, or do any of the much worse things that are daily publicized in the papers. Some of them do.

Most of them, however, quietly and in the most gentlemanly fashion imaginable, have retreated. Back and back from their original position as the leader and the head of the home, they have retreated, trying to recoup their losses at each step. They grow quiet in this defeat. Even at mixed parties the women toss the conversational ball. All too often the men congregate in small groups, coming alive only when they all talk shop. And there are few happy women. Very few.

The man's loss is the woman's loss. The modern wife, I deeply believe, is not happy because she *wants* to follow. She needs to follow. And there is nobody out ahead of her to lead the way. I do not believe that a woman wants, basically and instinctively, to hold the reins, to have complete charge of the home, often the money, with all the attendant annoyances, worries, and problems. She wants to help. She wants to share. But she never meant it to go so far that the major responsibilities fall upon her. She wants to have somebody to look up to, to tell her confidently, "Don't you fuss about it, dear. I'll take care of it."

Who is to solve it? I really don't know. But sometimes it seems as if the woman, taking the first step, asking the questions and listening with respect, helping her husband stand tall, has *real* power in her hands, *real* woman's liberation.

◦§ 41 ௰◦

THE ENERGY CRISIS

How are you making out in this "energy crisis" we hear so very much about? Is your sweater heavy enough to counteract the lower thermostat? Are you fighting restlessness as you stay home more instead of tooting about in your car? And are you weary of getting up in the dark and fumbling around for an hour or so before dawn comes? Well, that's one kind of energy we're all trying to conserve. But there are other ones.

Our friend Webster describes *energy* as "internal or inherent power; vigorous operation; power efficiently and forcibly exerted; capacity for performing work; emphasis." In turn, speaking of *power*, he calls it "the faculty of doing or performing something; ability; force; strength; rule or authority; dominion; government; influence; mental capacity; legal authority; ruler or sovereign; state or nation; supernatural being or agent; force tending to produce motion." Whew!

In the light of such descriptions, in the light of the talk all over the world about the *outside* energy crisis, I began to wonder about us—all of us—and whether or not we have an *inner* energy to work with.

You see, he mentions "inherent power." This we are born with, not only to make our bodies grow and move, but to develop our minds to their full capacities. Above all, it seems to me, to develop our *spiritual force* to its ultimate. There is no denying a spiritual force inside of each of us. But sometimes, when the outside world seems too tough to take, it gets buried, or lies dormant, or is lost altogether. Looking around at the people I know, searching myself some, I wonder if perhaps the loss of this spiritual power isn't perhaps the greatest crisis in energy that the world has to face.

Strength Webster calls energy, too. And here again, the inner comes into play. We have to have so terribly much strength today. Just to survive. Just to exist. Just to turn our hearts and minds away from the evils in the world—the pornography, the drugs, the liquor, the hopelessness. Just to polish ourselves a little, to have a little faith, to feel that the simple act of day-to-day living is worthwhile.

He calls power, for one definition, *dominion*. Probably he just means government dominion, but there is another kind of dominion which human beings have to hang on to like grim death. This is the dominion over *self*. The constant struggle to have the logical thinking mind rule the wild and unruly emotions. It's very easy to slip from grace in this department. And hard to climb back up and attain it.

Webster also mentions "supernatural being or agent" as part and parcel of power. Could we perhaps call "faith" part of the supernatural power of our lives? Could we feel that we are ruled—if we must be ruled by an outside source—by something we can't see or touch or even feel? By some real and lasting and forever power, which has created us from nothing and brought us from nowhere and set us here for such a very short time. To what purpose? To use for that brief moment the energy we were born with. To—again Webster—forcibly exert our capacity for performing work. To put the emphasis where it belongs. To maintain the faculty of doing or performing something? Could that be so?

Oh yes, we're all worried about keeping warm enough in cold weather, about running our cars on various errands and to work and vacations, about how we're going to push those many boats that sit in the marinas around in the sun all over the country.

But it seems to me, as I think about it, that our energy crisis has been with us—*innerly*—for a very long time. That slowly we have been using up and not replacing the energy of the *real* powers that we started out with. Spiritually, so far as mental, physical, and emotional strength are concerned, so far as controlling ourselves and our lives is concerned. So far, above all, as trusting in a final and great Power is concerned.

This is why people say we are apathetic. We've let our *outside* forces run through our fingers. But, more sadly, we've let our *inside* energy dribble away. We can let it all go and not care. Or we could, if we really tried, rebuild, restore, regain, what we were born to have.

᪥ 42 ᪥

OLD FOLKS AT HOME

A few days ago I went to visit a friend in one of those fine nursing homes. We had a good talk, and I managed to get almost all of the way out, keeping my glance straight ahead. I didn't peek into the private rooms, or private lives. I didn't want to see from each doorway the eager, painful swing of heads, the sharp, squashed hope on each old face that found me stranger. I paced quickly.

At the door I was stopped by an old man in a wheelchair. He raced it toward me. He looked up at me out of eyes covered with fog. He asked me in a voice as faint as far rain, "Will you kiss me, please?"

I did. And, thank God, I didn't hesitate.

But all of the rest of that day I walked with fury. I knew the old man, his son, his daughter-in-law, his proud, intelligent quartet of grandchildren. I knew their civic place, their big home, their social accomplishments. I knew, too, that the nurse stopped me at the door. She asked, "Will you come to see him again? Could you? Nobody comes to see him, ever, this poor old man. It's killing him."

Not his body dying, alone. That he could bear. His spirit, unwanted, discarded, no longer of use, dying in fragments because, in truth, there is no room for him at the inn. I am still angry!

The nursing home was beautifully graded and planted outside, immaculate and hushed inside. The nurses were kind and sunny. The food was excellent. For half an hour a day one of the nurses helped the old man to dress and took him for a wheelchair ride outdoors.

I remember a story I read when I was a child. It was about an old man who had no teeth. He made fierce noises when he ate. Those slurping sounds offended his family. So they put him in a corner with his back toward them and gave him his bowl of porridge to eat by himself.

When I was a child I was easily touched. The story hurt me. I wanted very much to sit down in the corner with the old man and share his gruel and talk to him while we ate together. Now I am no longer young, and not so easily moved. I say to myself, "Well, at least the family let him stay home. They gave him a roof over his head and cooked his food for him and let him sleep in a place where they were, where he could call out and be answered by a familiar voice."

To be at home, old and ill, is a big thing. Just to go to bed at night and know that in the other rooms around yours is your own family if you need them in the dark hours; to know even that should you die in your sleep, you have done so among friends and that no stranger will find you in the morning must be warmth and consolation for those whose years put them always within the close circle of death's nearness. To wake in the morning full of aches, pains, and confusion and be oriented by the sounds of grandchildren getting ready for school, son or daughter showering for the day, bright cooking smells coming from a home kitchen, can mean the difference between a day of living and a day of deep depression.

The nursing homes are filled with people like the little man. Sons, daughters, even grandchildren work overtime, use their savings, sometimes borrow to "give him the best." Phooey! To get him out of the way! Why?

Oh, they have reasons. House too small. Husband wants wife in the evening. Hard on the kids. The mother with her club, church, and bridge groups. The simple truth, though, is it costs too much, more than they can pay, in patience, kindliness, gentleness, firmness, time, strength. From the heart outward.

Our ancestors broke their backs to maintain their self-respect and considered a debt, no matter to whom, a thing to be paid first, before the beer and pianola. Their debt to their parents, aged and ill, or even to cousin spinsters was one they paid without considering themselves strained or noble. Mama and Papa and Aunt Eloise never belonged to the government. They belonged to son and daughter, even as at one time the situation had been reversed. No matter their dispositions, they were Mama and Papa and Aunt Eloise.

The schools cannot raise our children and set them close personal examples of unselfishness and decency. The government cannot pay our way to make our decisions for us as to patriotism, honesty, integrity. The churches cannot practice our religion for us. The libraries cannot pour knowledge into us. The scientists cannot design a heart for us. Teachers cannot give us pride. Space cannot show us true democracy. God himself cannot lift us above the level of the delicately constructed thinking, feeling animal.

We have to do it ourselves, don't we?

❧ 43 ❧

GOOD MORNING, GOD

Last year I started doing a strange thing. For me, at least. I started waking up and before my eyes were really opened, before I said hello to anybody else in the family, before my coffee and my deep breath for the day, I found myself saying, "Good morning, God."

I really don't want to scare any of you away with talk of prayer or religion. But that little daily greeting to the source of all power has begun to mean a lot to me and I'd like to share it.

I *can* share it because I started writing down the "Good mornings." For instance, day before yesterday, awake at last and alone for a second cup of coffee, I jotted down:

"Good morning, God. I give thanks this day. Not for any great and special thing. For opening my eyes, first of all, to see a clean familiar room around me.

"I give thanks for being able to stretch my length upon the

bed and pull on muscles that still answer my command. For the hot water and the soft soap with which to wash my face. For the slippers and robe, both shaped by my use, that take me to the kitchen. And the stove that turns at my touch to give me the strong steaming coffee that stirs me to action. I give thanks for the chair whereon I sit and the view from the window, with clean sun upon fresh snow. For the sounds of movement in the house and out. The milk truck coming down the street. The cough and humming of the refrigerator that holds the security of today's sustenance.

"I give thanks that on the desk there is a letter from a friend who waits to hear how it is with me. And on the table there is a book, half read, which calls to my mind. Thanks because sometime today I will hear a voice, in the store or post office or on the phone, greeting me in warmth. What a list, dear Lord, could we each make every morning if we tried."

That was one. Awhile back I was asked to say grace at a woman's club luncheon. I searched through all sorts of books trying to find one that would fit well. And finally I gave up and made up my own. I said:

"Dear Lord, you have brought us together today, knowing our need for human companionship, knowing that our minds and hearts are refreshed by our shared words, our shared aims, our shared activities.

"Bless these things that are common to us all as friends. But let us share, also, with thee, a higher companionship, a perpetual refreshment, from a source that has no limit.

"Dear Father, you have given us that tangible food and drink that is before us so that our bodies may move more strongly, our thoughts more clearly. But give us also, we pray thee sincerely, of that unseen food that is thy grace, of that quenching drink that is thy forgiveness and thy blessing.

"Bless, too, please God, the thoughts of our minds, the warmth of our hearts. Put thy hand gently on our lips whenever those thoughts or that warmth, grow tipped with pettiness and frosted with unkindness.

"Above all, Lord, make us always and forever hungry and thirsty for the total meaning and comprehension of thee. We ask it in thy Son's name. Amen."

Sometimes I think that prayer is a habit, one which can conquer the habits of worry and fear, of which we've had too much. You can use it anywhere. In the kitchen, "Dear God, let me make a good cake for Johnny's birthday." In the bathroom, "Dear God, let me keep my own choppers until I'm an old lady." In the living room, "Dear God, let me manage my day so that I can read something and get my rusty mind working again." In the bedroom, "Thank you, God, for the way I fall asleep so quickly after a busy day."

And out of the house, too. As we pass a hospital, "Take care of them, and give them health again, and spare me, please, for my duties." As we read the paper. As we kiss the kids good-bye. As we watch an old man get on a bus. As we look. As we live. "Dear God, please." "Dear God, thank you."

Seems small, maybe. Perhaps. Perhaps.

Anyway this whole thing started because a letter came from a stranger the other day. It ended, "May God be with you always." Somehow, I had never felt better, even after a benediction in church.

⊸§ 44 §⊷

THE FOOLISH FORTIES

I was thinking—and don't ask me how or why, because I don't know—about Jack Benny the other day. Remember how he was always thirty-nine? And it amused us. It made us laugh because we know how he felt, or was pretending to feel. Reader identification—only visual. Thirty-nine sounds fine and dandy. Forty sounds terrible!

I expect all of us have hit upon that story of the woman who leans forward toward her mirror and suddenly, shockingly, sees dozens of gray strands in her glossy dark hair. And notes around the eyes, the mouth, the fine sprays of wrinkles beginning to etch themselves. How does she always feel in the story? She feels numb, caught in the illusion of age. And she senses the frail, withered ghost of a time to come. "Forty," she mutters desperately. "Forty," she sobs.

Sounds silly, doesn't it? But it, or something like it, comes to all of us. And we acknowledge it, one way or another. But never, not ever, with welcome and pleasure, as an honored guest. It seems a shameful admission to make about us, but I do believe that if we had our way completely, we would stay thirty-nine forever along with Benny.

Why do we feel this way? Primarily, I suppose, because there is such a violent accent, such a barrage of pressure, upon the glory of youth in America. Not only upon youth itself, but upon staying youthful forever and ever, and well beyond. Superficial attractiveness, lack of wrinkles, lack of expression, lack of bulges, lack of weariness, lack of nervousness—it comes to us from all directions, in all sorts of advertisements, TV programs, articles.

If we would give to the development of our personalities, the stretch of our minds, the growth of our spirits, the search for our inner selves, if we would give just half the time and attention and thought we, as women, give to the waves of our hair, the creams on our faces, the uplift of our bosoms, and the balancing of our diet, there would be a revolution of sorts.

We would be so gracious, so filled with realness, so serene

in self-understanding, so well read and even wise that we would pull everybody to us, even our husbands of years, and hold them tight. And nobody would notice whether we plucked our eyebrows to a flawless seductive arc, used Worship Me nail polish and lipstick, or weighed twenty pounds more than we should.

Seriously, though, the forties do bring fear, as youth seems behind us. We have now lived, probably, longer than we have yet to live. Besides, there is another knowledge. We may have reached our nearer horizons, but the far ones of our younger dreams are still foggy in the distance. And we begin to see that our abilities were never as great as we once hoped they would be. And last, there is a little broken music box that plays out the whir of the days—shorter years, seasons running a relay race more quickly than ever before.

If we can see these things and destroy them before they destroy us, we can manage to sail through the forties and enjoy those years.

The dangerous age. Newspapers, books, stories, the divorce courts, too often give the account of these years. They all tell of one general feeling. The nasty sensation that we've missed something. Too many, propelled by this emotion, move suddenly crashward in their lives, imbued with the idea that somewhere along the line, that which was intangible and lovely beyond expression slipped away from them without their knowing it. So they try to catch it.

It's not safe to look around too much in the forties. Not even those closest to us can bear much scrutiny at this time. Our children have grown tall and independent. To look at them is to feel older, used up, our vocation outmoded. Our partner is tired, a little gray, a little lined, and probably a little short-tempered. To look at him (or her) is to feel the contrast that breaks the heart, to remember when we were both so young, fresh, forward looking together, that era ago.

There's nothing for the forties but to look inside. Quite a few surprise packages can be waiting for us. The proven understanding of many words we didn't know when young: Compromise. Patience. Close horizons. Comfort. Safety. Accomplishment. Time for more. Health. Balance. Mental authority. Make your own list.

The pain of the forties is real, like physical pain. But if it is borne with patience; with some degree of courage; with quiet, closed lips and a little pride, dignity, and a strong mind; it will heal of itself.

✑ 45 ✑

YOUR HEART TO A DOG

Two friends of mine got puppies for Christmas this year. One of them (the friends, I mean, not the pup) was eight years old. The other was a retired woman who lived alone. The little girl received a cockapoo, part poodle, part cocker, wholly enchanting. The woman friend has what she calls a springle. Part springer, part beagle. Equally enchanting.

Somebody once said, "Don't give your heart to a dog to break." It is a sentence that rolls easily off the tongue. But it doesn't bear much thinking about. It is as if somebody had said, "Don't ever fall in love. Or marry. Or have children. Or make friends. Because something might happen to separate you from those you care for. And you'd be hurt."

One time, a long while ago, the express man carried a large box carefully up to the side door of a boarding house. He balanced it against one knee and rang the bell. The door was opened by a gray-haired man who looked as if he had been waiting for the box to arrive. He didn't say anything, just paid the express man, and lifted the box very gently into his own arms.

96

When the door shut, the man carried the box to the kitchen. There were three people waiting in that kitchen. A young woman, an older woman, and a young man. They just stood in a circle and stared at the box.

The gray-haired man set the box down. "Let's just watch to see what he does," he said.

With the sound of his voice, howling and whimpering and barking came in rapid succession from the box.

"Bangie," the older woman cried. "My Bangie."

So they stood, four grown people, with tears running down their cheeks, while the box was opened and a small white dog returned to them. Returned to them with a flurry of tail and a scurry of feet, with licking and whining and barks of joy. And, somehow, although those four people no longer had a home and had left all their friends behind them, they grew warm and comforted from the joyous welcome.

And when, at long last, when he was eighteen years old, that little white dog died, of course there was mourning. But the loyalty and friendship and love he had given through his life more than made up for the heartbreak.

So I am pleased for my young friend and my older friend and their Christmas gifts. Of course, they both have a problem on their hands. They can rest assured that there is never going to be a dull moment, at least until the dog grows old and weary and wants nothing better than a soft bed under the stove. But one thing is true for both of them: The days of wondering just what life is all about, or the long moments of boredom, or the lonely evenings because the children are all grown up (or perhaps a strange city, or widowhood) are gone forever.

Because a dog is more than fun. He sort of makes you a psychologist, you know? Trying to understand him—from the five-dollar purchase of the runt of the litter down the street to a much extolled, highly pedigreed AKC selection—is as stimulating to the mind as his ownership is gratifying to your heart. You can get as much, or as little, mental lift from a dog as you have eyes to see, ears to hear, and understanding to comprehend.

It's impossible to tell, of course, what, in general, any dog's reaction to a given situation will be. But reactions there are, from the youngest to the oldest. Some of them you just watch and try to comprehend. Others you understand, with a catch in your throat or an amused chuckle. At any rate, they keep you from thinking too much of the exterior problems of the day, and the interior problems of yourself.

Now see what I've done. I've talked myself right into dog hunger, considering that our last lost lamented has been gone five years. Wonder if I'm too old to try again? Well, anyhow, I think I'll call my older friend and invite myself to tea this afternoon. That springle is really something!

⋖§ 46 §⋗

ALL THE LONELY PEOPLE

I sat in a small restaurant recently, sipping coffee and, being lucky me, waiting for my husband to join me for lunch. When I am by myself like that, I have to admit, I am a Peeping Thomasina and an eavesdropper.

All around me that day, it seemed, there were women eating alone and men eating alone. They kept holding up the friendly waitress, talking to her as long as she would hold still for them, even complaining some in order to get and keep her attention. And I began to think of loneliness.

There is a difference, you know, between being alone and being lonely, isn't there? To be alone means just to be apart from others, single, only, solely. To be alone is a very good thing for all of us, once in a while. To give ourselves the refreshment of some sort of meditation, to write the careful, thoughtful letter, to read the magazine we've been waiting to be alone to explore, to sew with concentration, or finish up a piece of intricate counted knitting or delicate needlepoint, to take a walk, tasting everything you look at in memory, in delight. That's a good thing, being alone that way.

To be lonely is quite another deal. "All the lonely people," I thought that day in the restaurant, and it hurt a little to think of them. Because to be lonely means that you are not alone on purpose. Circumstances and life have forced you to be, right? Loneliness is to feel deserted, to feel solitary, alienated, like an unfrequented and abandoned house. And it is a terrible emotion to bear day after day, year after year.

There are some things to counteract loneliness, though. I know from observations, and from the infrequent but desperate times when I, myself, have known it. Many older wives, many widows, and those of every age whose husbands travel, often complain of feeling lonely or useless. Other wives, and widows too, similarly placed, lead full lives and enjoy every minute. There are some questions for the lonely ones to ask themselves in order to know to which group they belong:

Do you read a daily newspaper? Attend church regularly? Occasionally baby-sit for a friend? Read a new book every month? Take part in some community activity? Try a new recipe quite often? Write at least two letters a week? Call on neighborhood newcomers? Note funny things to tell people or relatives you know? Plan an occasional surprise for those friends and relations? Regularly read a woman's magazine? Spend one evening a week socially? Follow a hobby that you enjoy? Have at least one close friend?

If you score as well as the average wife or even widow, the number of your *yes* answers will total ten to twelve. Mothers of small children, who, believe me, can be as lonely in the

midst of daily hubbub as the older ones who live by themselves, often score one or two points less. Then the bored,
childless, or lonely wife, the bored woman whose husband
has died and whose children live somewhere else, whatever
her age, usually scores eight or less. Regardless of your score,
if you feel left out or unwanted, maybe your *no* answers will
suggest ways you can have a richer life.

It's not easy to do, I know, but the best of all ways not to
be lonely is not to live too much within the confines of your
memories of better times. As I've said, it's contrast that breaks
the heart. And acceptance of a present time of aloneness will
make real loneliness fade away. There is so much in all of us,
so much potential for all the things we earlier in life never
did, that every day can be a sort of reaching outward toward
other people, toward new activities, toward the very act of
living itself.

A very cynical person said once that "Life is easier than
you think. All you have to do is accept the impossible, do
without the indispensable, and bear the intolerable." That's a
sarcasm against life, isn't it? But a better, if somewhat bitter
description of it is that "In life you have to forget the un-
forgettable and forgive the unforgivable." It sounds rugged.
But if you can do that, even in a small way, about life's in-
justices, such as the fact that you are both alone and lonely,
it's possible to pick up your daily routine and enlarge and
strengthen it.

At least I deeply hope it is, since I know that I really enjoy
being alone, but pray that I'll never be really lonely.

◄§ 47 §►

THE LOVELY TWENTIES

Do you remember what it was like to be in your twenties? It
isn't easy to remember innocence. It isn't easy to recall

gaiety. It's not simple to sense adventure again. It's not simple to regain tenderness. Yet, when we were twenty, these qualities were ours. They were the gifts of material that life gave to us. We fashioned them, you and I, into a bright, swinging cloak to fly gracefully in the breeze as we ran to our future.

The first job I, in my twenties, won during the depression was clerking on the main floor of a large department store. I sold gloves and a center-counter "special" on peanuts, and there were nine dollars in my pay envelope at the end of the week.

The third day I was late, caught in traffic. There was no time to go up to the employees' cloakroom. I left my coat and scarf and hat on a hook in the basement and took the freight elevator to my main-floor station.

When the long, peanut-studded day was over, I went back for my things. The cellar was dark, gloomy—and empty. Empty of workers, and more. Empty of my coat, hat, scarf. I looked all over. They were gone.

The freight elevator man called from his cage, "Come on, girlie. For Pete's sake, before we both get locked in."

I ran back. "My coat and hat are gone. They've been stolen, I think."

"That was a good bright trick," he consoled me. He opened the doors at the main floor. "You can kiss them good-bye."

I walked to the one open door with the guard who checked us for stolen packages. Beyond him the rain came straight down, determined and cold and gray. I started out the door. The guard looked at me curiously. A voice yelled at me, hollow in the empty store. "Wait a minute, girlie," it cried. I stopped.

The freight elevator man came up. He had a battered hat on his round head, a mackinaw on his shoulders, and a black sweater over his arm. "Wear this," he proffered. "You can't go out without something. Wear my sweater."

He held it out. I took it. It was slippery with grease. I put it on. The warmth of him was still in it, a dirty, kindly warmth that took the chill out of me at once.

The guard spoke up. "I got a clean handkerchief you could put over your head," he offered cautiously. He pulled it out of his pocket, a red and white bandanna. I tied it under my chin. I tipped my head. I held the corners of the sweater out like the ruffles of a ballet skirt. I twirled. The elevator man laughed. The guard joined him. I found my own laughter running to meet theirs.

"Goodnight, boys," I called and threw myself out into the wind, the rain, and the cold. I could smell myself all the way home on the bus. A greasy, long-worn odor combined with a chewing-tobacco smell from the back-pocket home of the kerchief. People stared at me, I suppose. I must have been a sight in my black dress with the frills left over from better days, and the sweater and the bandanna.

But I didn't mind. Somebody in that store had cared whether I got pneumonia or not, had cared enough to do something about it.

Years later, whenever I went into that department store, I rode the freight elevator. Pat his name was, and he had a wife and six kids. They practically lived on vegetable soup. I knew, because I went there for supper one night. I had a wonderful time.

I am glad to sniff that old sweater, that bus oil, the rain, the tobacco, all these many many years later. Perhaps you have to grow old to remember, to know, that innocence, gaiety, adventure, and tenderness were all part of your life when you were in your twenties. You, too?

48

WHERE ARE THE SHEPHERDS?

After my mother died, when the funeral was over, I sat quietly staring out my window at a slow dawn, and a strange question came into my mind. Strange to me, at least.

"Where are the shepherds?" it asked.

It was a lovely funeral. The chapel was rimmed with soft organ music. The flowers papered the walls and stood in halos of brilliance. Over the shimmering gray of the casket lay a blanket of roses as thick as eiderdown.

The minister stood before the raised podium, tall, with a soft, clear voice. He told of my mother's long, good life. Of the promise that had now been kept. Of the joy everlasting that had now been received. He spoke of eternity. He spoke of her and her dedication.

I hoped, staring out of my window in the early morning, that my mother had heard his eulogy. Because she most certainly hadn't heard any of those words while she was still living. Three years ill, too proud to beg the minister to come calling, she always excused him with, "He's a busy man. It's a big church."

The minister did come three times. Once when we relayed my mother's sudden illness. Twice more, at our insistence in the bad times. Once a year, for an old lady who had been a "deaconess" and whose world was her church.

Where are the shepherds?

The poor clergy. Like a huge spiritual pie, they are cut into such slim slices that it is a wonder that they go around at all. Convocations, conferences, canvasses. Vestry, church schools, confirmations, missions. Church suppers, young people's groups, adult Sunday School, memorial services, funerals, weddings. Visiting dignitaries, prayer groups, guild teas, rummage sales. In their studies working out sermons to aid the human spirit a little on Sunday. Hardly time, late at night, to drop to their knees in prayers for strength, or read over a beloved passage in their Bible.

The trouble with being cut so fine, of course, is that the juice, the rich content of the filling, has a chance to slither away, and there is no nourishment and very little flavor left in the superficial crust.

To be a shepherd is to be one who tends sheep, a pastor, to tend as a shepherd. To tend.

It seems to me, with all my fondness for ministers, that the time has come for men of the cloth to hunt for that sheep who strayed from Sunday service. To nurse that lamb who is ailing. To give warmth to the dying sheep. To know each one separately. Not by a name, a pat once a week, but by the curl of its wool, its needs, its disposition. The time has come for pastors everywhere to walk with the crook of their dedication in their hands, in and out, closely, of the herd they were given to keep.

Christ, in his time on earth, walked everywhere, talked to everyone, inspired and healed, healed, healed. He was not always on the Mount, speaking in majesty and glory. As often he was in the valley, walking the highways and byways, the dust of the world on his feet identical to that on those of his following.

The diseases of our day are not visible on the skin or even in the mind. The cancer of alienation, the leprosy of fear, the palsy of indecision, the blindness of materialism, the limp of disillusion. Christ is not here to lay his hand upon those diseases and cure them. But his ministers are.

There are millions of destructive people alive in the world. There are more millions of positive believing men and

women of good will. But they must be led, cared for, suc-
cored, so that their strength can grow to match and surpass
the darker forces. Who is to lead them if not the men of God?

This is a time for healing, for inspiration, for mingling, for
stepping down from the Mount into all the valleys. To build
a temple and fill it with three services a Sunday is a fine
thing. To build a soul, or mend one, or find one, or heal one,
is a far greater accomplishment. To add one such integrated
soul to another is to create a world congregation that no evil
can defeat.

Where *are* the shepherds?

⋽ 49 ⋻

A SEARCH FOR QUIET

The other day I got caught up in a really good book. Heaven
knows they're rare enough nowadays. It's really a chore and
a challenge to go to the library and pick out several slabs of
fiction, to go home with that little lift that having something
to read has always given us. But it's a sore disappointment to
find within the first chapter all the dirty words that used to be
written on sidewalks and all the shocking situations that were
never mentioned except behind closed doors, or not at all.

What happened with that interesting book that pushed me
on from page to page, turning each one eagerly, is that I kept
trying to find a quiet place to read it. I'd been fairly busy all
day, and when the dinner dishes were done, I sat down in the
living room, in a comfortable chair with a footstool and the
table lamp coming just right over my left shoulder.

I jumped a mile when the stereo in the big alcove that is
part of said living room began to bleat. Now, the stereo
belongs to our visiting son, and it is, I sometimes think, as

dear as life to him. At least, until all the rest of the payments are made. Usually it plays really beautiful classic records from his large collection of the same. But his interest also extends to include what he calls "soft rock." Some of it is not too bad, really, if you can just accustom yourself to the volume, which he claims he turns down ridiculously low for the sake of his poor old parents. Anyhow, there I was in the middle of a sentence, and my heart jumped to my throat, my body jumped a foot off the chair, and I forgot what I was reading.

Well, he hasn't been home long, and after all, it is his basic place of residence and security, so I smiled at him, listening and reading, and staggered up the stairs to the wild accompaniment of that terrible monotonous bass that is my primary argument against rock. I shut the big strong door at the top and thought, "Well, I'll just go into my nice front bedroom and get going on my book again."

I walked in there, and lo, my husband, who loves TV as much as his family, I believe, was leaning forward watching some wild and woolly shooting—again with volume—on a Western. So, I thought, trying also to smile at him, I'll just go into the back bedroom.

That was a mistake. Even with doors closed, the heavy popping of guns and the heavy thump of rock destroyed what concentration I still have left at my age. All of a sudden I got the feeling that if one more gun exploded, one more bad man writhed in the dust, one more horse galloped gloriously over the piled rocks and narrow trails, I got the feeling if one more tinny tremolo voice was framed in electronic instruments of great strength, even if one more opera were played full force in our house—a house, mind you—I would flip! Blow. Go off my rocker, or go bananas, as the kids say nowadays. You've got to have a quiet moment sometimes.

Well, I can tell you where to get it. Just take an evening walk around the block.

Know what? You won't see a soul. Not a human being. Maybe a car full of kids will roar down the street, or a slower one will cruise by, its occupants staring at you curiously as though you were a freak as they try to find a house number among the black, unlit domiciles. But you, and your dog if you have one, own the world at night. If the shades aren't drawn, you can see the gray flickers. Usually can't see householders, though. They're on the floor or on the davenport or on a low chair out of range. No matter what else they're on, it's for sure the base of their spines, primarily. Callouses in delicate places. Like the spine. Like the mind?

Ray Bradbury wrote a short story once about a man who took a walk at night and was arrested by a robot police car for doing such an odd and nonconforming thing. This was about the year 2000. It scared me when I read it. And it scared me to walk around the block, too. I began to remember all the muggings and shootings and such I'd read in the paper. I began to hurry and at last I was running up the silent, empty walk—just as, believe it or not, a police car slowed down and I was thoroughly stared at.

I opened the door. There I was, safe again. BANG, BANG, BOOM, BOOM, SLAM—TAKE THAT! DRAW! OOMPA OOMPA RAINDROPS KEEP FALLING THUMP THUMP OOMPA OOMPA.

It was nice outdoors, just the same, with the evening's hint of spring to come. Awful lonely, though.

◅§ 50 §▻

THE BIG FOOTSTEPS

They said that it was the coldest winter Rochester, New York, had ever known—back then in the year 1933. I had a "transient" job, usually held only by those who worked awhile until they could get enough for a drinking spree and move on. I worked for a newspaper, at the bottom below the bottom. Each day I took a trolley to the coldest suburb of the city, near the lake. Each day, battling through snow to my thighs, I pushed my way up to the big houses and gave them an argument as to why they should sample—free—an unpopular paper for two weeks. If they agreed, I was back again, in the snow, the ice, against the freezing wind, to talk them into a subscription.

Back then I was constantly cold. I froze one foot. I walked in an inner daze, in woolen panties, hose, double sweaters, my lover's football sweater, my one good coat, and my mother's wool-lined gloves salvaged fron the chaos of losing everything.

Doors slammed in my face or nobody answered. I was frozen inside, too. All the philosophy, the religious beliefs, the optimism I'd lived with all my life, were like icicles hanging in my mind and heart. And they never melted.

The baker man was a stopgap. He'd halt and say, "See that big green tree over there? I'll meet you at lunch time and we'll have a sandwich and a cold beer and get out of this terrible heat." Sometimes he gave me a cookie or two, and I ate it carefully, knowing that any saliva would freeze at the corners of my mouth.

Then one day I met a postman coming out of a house I was, hopefully, about to enter. He stood stock still and stared at me. "What," he asked slowly, "are you doing out in this weather?" I told him.

For a long moment he looked down at me with a kind of tenderness. Then he said, "Listen, sweetie, this snow is so thick, so hard to push your way through. You'll never make it alone through the winter. But I tell you what I'll do. From now on I'll make big footsteps. I'll slide my feet a little. I'll make a path for you. I'll clear the way as much as I can. I'll show you how to go."

He turned abruptly and started to move away. He did just what he'd said he'd do. He scraped his feet, and opened a place where I could walk, not comfortably perhaps, but more easily and safely.

I was very still watching him go down the street, watching him turn into each house, looking down at the clearance he had made for me, going before me, helping me, almost shoveling the way, with his big feet in their great boots. I watched him for a long time, until he grew small in the distance. Despite the grayness of the day and the spitting snow, there seemed to be a light—like sunshine around his head. I never saw him again, that postman. But there was always a narrow path down which I could make my way.

In the years since then, when life is thick and hard to push through, I think about the postman with that light around his head. I think about the path he cleared for me.

I trusted his word. The big footsteps. "I'll make a path for you. I'll clear the way. I'll show you how to go."

All those years, when the symbolic winter was bitter, when my heart was cold, when I was alone and desperate, I held still. I stopped pushing my own way. I learned to *let go*. And never once did it fail that there was a path opened where I could walk in safety and in the direction that was for my own benefit and protection.

Opened by whom? I don't put a name to it. But isn't it strange? For all of us perhaps—a path opened.

⋖§ 51 §⋗

THE OLD COUPLE

During the war they now call the "Second" we lived with an old couple, sharing their home and kitchen privileges. The little old lady weighed about ninety pounds. The old man had once been tall, but he was bent over and shaky and his legs were wrapped in bandages. Both of them were practically confined to the circumference of their house, the backyard, and the grocery store half a block down the street.

They had lived together a long time, those two. Raised three kids, given them good educations, let them scatter, and didn't ask anything of anybody. Except of each other. Oh, they nipped at each other sometimes. Especially when the cherry tree was hanging heavy.

That's when Elgar insisted on picking every last cherry. He got out the ladder, and that was a major project. He set it up firmly against the tree, and that was a second great effort. He tied a big pan around his neck, and that took a while, too, because his hands were swollen and slow. Then he climbed the ladder and hid his face among the leaves and the shining deep crimson clusters of cherries. That was the greatest effort of them all.

The first few hours Ella didn't mind. She got all the pots and kettles out and set them around the kitchen. She measured the hoarded sugar. As Elgar brought the cherries in, she pitted them, washed them, and started to preserve, to can, to make jam and jelly. The sun was hot and the weather muggy in the season when the cherries were ripe. The kitchen was Hades with a linoleum floor. Ella's white hair turned flat and scrawny. Her busy little feet slowed hour after hour. But still the cherries came. Buckets of them.

That old man with bandages on his legs was a demon. All the first day, the second, the third, up he went, there he stayed, down he came, and in went the cherries to the kitchen. By the end of the second day, Ella was completely undone every time he kicked the screen with his foot. "There's no keeping up with you," she cried. "Let the birds have a few. Give them to the neighbors. I'm tons behind you." He shook his head and peered over his glasses. "Waste not, want not," he admonished. And back to the tree he went.

It was a hard time in the old gray house. It was a bad time for the old marriage. I was young; it seemed to me that by the time you reached your seventies, there ought to be a glorious sort of serenity in marriage, and calm and complete understanding, a perfect give and take.

When the cherries were all gone from the tree, when every last one had been brought in by those swollen hands and those shuffling feet, when all the sugar had been used (and five pounds of mine, too) they asked me to look. They stood together in the kitchen and waited for me to admire. It was an admirable sight. All the flat surfaces, the sink, stove, breakfast nook, cupboards, and dining-room table were bedecked and packed with shimmering jars and glasses. It was enough for a family of ten simply crazy for cherries, and for two years. It was funny, considering how many other jars from other years there were down in the cellar.

I laughed about it sometimes. But after we were away from that simple gray house, whenever the cherry season came along, I used to stop for a minute. I used to say a little prayer that Elgar was still climbing up into that tree and that Ella was rushing and perspiring and maybe even cursing softly to keep up with those silver bubbles on top of the red richness in all those pans.

You see, I couldn't quite forget the way the two of them looked down in the storage cellar, with one overhead light cutting across the pride on their faces, when the last jar was put away. I was remembering the way they forgot me and turned to each other and reached out simultaneous hands, and smiled almost identical smiles. "Well," Elgar said. "Yes," Ella echoed.

I still think of them at cherry time, although they have been dead for a long time. I realize now that the cherry tree was a challenge and a symbol. I hope very much that they managed to meet that challenge every year until the very last. It was something they accomplished together in years so circumscribed that there wasn't much they could do any longer. Elgar set himself to manhood and danger when he climbed that tree. He urged Ella on, as he must often have urged her through hard, busy younger times. And Ella kept up. Struggling, angry, and deploring his masculine stubbornness. But she kept up. And worked with him—and created something with him. And they shared the victory.

That, my friends, is marriage.

⋅⒮ 52 ⒭⋅

SECURITY

One of the nice things about our modern life is that at sixty-five, or even at sixty-two if you choose, you can get your Social Security checks. Right? It would be nice if they were so fat that you didn't have to worry about a thing, but it's good in any case. Of course, now I'm giving away my advanced age, but I have to start somewhere, and I've been thinking lately about security of all kinds. Especially of what I term in my mind "The Us Generation."

It's always seemed strange to me the way each generation, really less than a generation, eight or ten years or so between, seems to think that they are the first to discover the world. One thing is certain. They each discover a different world and have very different problems to cope with. How they cope with them is what, of course, determines their character and their hope for any kind of future.

For a long time while I was growing older year by year, I felt very sorry for all of us who are now getting really old.

Everything seemed to pile in on us. We faced the depression, just got started at jobs that paid some fourteen dollars a week to start—then whoops! We were still young enough for the Second World War. Some of you had sons old enough for Korea, or some still young enough for Vietnam. That's just counting the wars, of course, and not all the varying tensions that popped up in between.

Our generation, we who *really* count the years in decades, who are now the grandparents and the old-fashioned ones, were good, obedient children. I don't mean that we minded our parents at all times. But somehow, because of the economic situation of the world, it never occurred to us not to do what was put in front of us. We listened to the golden voice of FDR and let it ease us. We looked at the sadness of our own lost parents and tried to ease them. We were afraid much of the time, but we felt that our obligation to swallow that fear, not even to acknowledge it, was necessary. We plowed ahead.

There is much fear abroad today, of course. More, in some ways than we knew. It is a different kind of fear. Ours, you see, was personal, was daily survival, and it made for all kinds of very fine relationships. Everybody was in the same boat, and when it rocked wildly, we all hung on together. We did everything together, especially the things that didn't cost any money, and our fears were close, personal ones, weren't they? Reminds me a little of the time the lights went out in New York. Suddenly, everybody was helping everybody else, and behold! There was not even any increase in crime. Our younger days were like that.

So now that I am much older, I no longer feel sorry for "The Us Generation." I think what we learned was very important and has been lost to the younger ones in the shuffle over the years. I expect, although I really don't want to admit it, that we are the last generation to feel and live many of the most important things. A sense of obligation to our parents. A feeling that we can manage to cope no matter what comes along, no matter how much it takes out of us emotionally. The knowledge that if one job ends, another can be found. The feeling of the so-called "sanctity of marriage." The tremendous importance of the family unit. The belief, now lost even to us, most likely, that our country was honest and straightforward and that it could manage to survive any disaster, as we survived our own.

I feel very sorry (don't you?) for the young ones today. Their fears, acknowledged or not, are so strange and vague, like the H-bomb hovering over their lives. Their search is so inner, so self-oriented, that they don't have the real joy that we did in looking outward to other people, in realizing that to lose the sense of self-analysis in the trying to understand those around you is truly to find yourself.

In more minor areas we've had it better, too. We liked to look neat, well groomed, and, as Archie Bunker and Edith sing, "Boys were boys and girls were girls." I love that nostalgic song. We thought good manners were important too, and there's still nothing wrong with them.

So, we really didn't have as bad a time as we thought we did at the time, if you know what I mean. I wouldn't be twenty again if I were paid enormously for it. Instead I'll be my doddering self, with my wonderful doddering friends, and that's *my* security—social and otherwise.

৺ঔ 53 ঔ৶

THIS IS MY LAND

Do you have an attic in your house? We do. And it's pretty big and pretty full. Not only of furniture from generations past, but piled high with cartons of books for which there is no room downstairs, and records the same. And, of course, in my case, with yellowing pages of the millions of words I've put on paper over the years. Everytime I go up there to search for something I might find useful for this little book, I can't find it. But I find something else.

Way back then, before anybody dreamed of what was going to happen to America as it is today, I worked for a radio station in Rochester, New York, even before World War II. We had a good-sized orchestra, and sometimes we didn't know what to do with it. So I concocted a program called "This Is My Land." Had a chorus behind it, too, and the narrator read out my words.

I found them, the other day. They seem young, of course, but they also seem to typify an attitude I deeply hope we'll all regain someday.

For instance, one program said: "Once upon a time my America was wilderness and savage. Slowly my people came, walking with a steady tread into the land. Slowly they planted and reaped the harvest of their hands and toil. Slowly they made paths across the country, roads for those who came still later to tread upon. Homes clung fiercely to the earth. Children were born and they grew up and died. And everywhere they left their mark upon my America. Men sat down with thoughts upon them and pondered and drew diagrams. The things they penciled became realities, schools, churches, strong square buildings. Men traded with each other and trusted, and found means to thwart the cold and hunger. It all started with a dream. And the dream was bred and sinewed into the men and women and into their children's children even to today. The dream is now."

How I wish it were! And another: "In my America there is a place called Washington. And there, as to a shrine, my people come. The sound of their feet is the wash of an ocean upon a shore, a murmuring shuffle that rises up the broad stairs to hush in sudden quiet before the molded symbol of a man who gave to them a freedom, tangible and warm. They stand there, my people, in the purple-lofted dusk, their spines grow taut with pride, their eyes wet with tears. They read the words carved into stone, the breathing words, 'Conceived in Liberty.' They look upon his face, angled and planed by light and shadow. Was he so different then, this great and simple man? Are not we the same? Small happiness, large sorrow, firm belief. The same? And courage, too, is that the same? No different now than then. An age does not separate man from man. And that which is born free, lives from century to century and does not know the meaning of the grave." How hopeful, yes?

Still another read: "A country without faith is a lamp without a wick. There is no light. In my America the lamps of faith are shining brightly in every window. Do you know what Sunday morning is, in my land? Can you dream of sunlight, golden, rich? Of little towns with picket fences round the yards? Of cities, rushing full of all of us? Of lonely places with narrow roads to lead them forth? To lead them forth, all of the people, men and women, children too. Forth they come from their daily lives, hand in hand with starched white collars and with crisp, clean dresses, forth they come together to their churches. All kinds of churches, heavy with endowment, pointed high with crosses, or small and white and neat. All kinds of faiths. Mennonite and Catholic, Lutheran and Puritan, forth they come to worship, as they feel it, as they please, in my America. Yes, no matter what great things I may tell you of my land, it would be less than a continent of dust, were it not for these beliefs." Is that lost, I wonder?

"From the beginning in my land," for instance it goes on, "my people have felt the stirring of spring in their hearts. Locked tight in snow and cold for many months, my country suddenly opens its arms to the rush and foam of rivers freed of ice, the long-remembering twilight, and the shy, sweet air that touches the cheek in quick caress. The feeling of spring is with my people all the winter long. No matter how bitter the wind may be, they know, in certainty, that it will pass. It is that way in their lives, too, a stretching to tomorrow which has given them their strength, a surety that after dark comes light, after pain there is peace, and after cold, warmth."

Young thoughts, young writing, oh yes. But if we were to pray, perhaps, some strange hard way, we could feel that they were about our land again.

❧ 54 ☙

LOVE THY NEIGHBOR?

Did you ever truly seriously think about the meaning of the word *neighbor*? Webster says, "A neighbor is one who dwells near to another. An intimate." Well, in this day and age, dwelling near to one another is a physical fact. In crowded apartments, on street after street in housing developments, in duplexes. But being "intimate" with our neighbors is seldom included in such near dwelling.

You know, when you really explore the word *intimate*, it begins to have all sorts of special meanings. But one, perhaps the most important, is the fact that intimacy is surely part of all love. So maybe that's something to think about.

Take the woman across the street, the one we shake our heads over because she screams at her children all the time and slams doors and never sounds anything but angry. We watch her come and go. See those big loads of washing? The defeated slope of her shoulders? The way she shuffles as she walks? And the porch light. So many nights a dim beacon on our dark street, waiting for her husband to pull in the drive?

We can begin to love her, can't we, as we see how it is with her? As we realize her burdens and our own contrasting good fortune.

But it isn't quite enough, just as it isn't enough loving your husband without ever telling him so. Or telling him so without ever showing it.

Perhaps we can even begin to do something for the woman across the street, in the light of our new approach to neighbors. Even if it is just inviting her over for a morning coffee break. Just giving her a chance to open up a little, by the warmth of our welcome and the expression in our eyes. Sure, sure, it takes time. It's inconvenient. She's nobody we would ordinarily really want to know. But perhaps, just maybe, we could search a little for a way to walk that is new to us.

The gossipy old lady. The couple who seem to hate kids. The neighborhood faultfinder. The boy with the quick fists. The man who speaks to nobody. Every street has them all. You know something? We can have them all, help them all, even love them all. If we honestly try. So, why don't we try to take our inner love out of the house a little and find places where it belongs?

There is, also, a harder, more difficult finding. Almost impossible, but the true refinement of love. We must cross an abyss for it. The chasms have many names. Intolerance. Prejudice. Resentment. Hate. Contempt. Pride. The list is as long as humanity's failings.

It is no simple matter to trail your compassion, your love, like a banner, across the abyss of hate. It is no simple matter to land on your feet on the other side and lift that banner high.

To care for those who are your enemies, those who revile you, those who are full of evil, those who are different from you in every possible way, those who have hurt you or your reputation, those who by touching you may soil you, is almost beyond our power to conceive. But if we truly try to "love our neighbor as ourself," when we do, it makes all the terrible falls into the chasms worth the bruises.

The second commandment, then, for us, the women, the simple ones (and yes, the men too), can begin with trying to walk in another man's shoes. It can go on from there to loving our families as we love ourselves. It can reach beyond four walls to encompass our neighbors and our friends. And it can, with a lifetime of effort, show us how to love our enemies.

What a project to think about, my friends. Indifferent, bored, lonely, alienated, self-pitying, whatever we are at different times. What a project to work on. Even if we never get beyond the lowliest brick in what must be a heaven-reaching cathedral.

Like the story of the two men, remember? Someone asked the first, watching him work, "What are you doing?" He answered, "I'm mortaring bricks together." The second one, when asked what he was doing, looked toward the sky and said simply, "I'm building a cathedral."

And so can we.

ৰ্কই 55 ই৵

WHAT ABOUT GUILT?

It seems to me sometimes that there is a great deal of sub-conscious guilt running around in the world today. A good amount of it is well-deserved for all sorts of crimes against each other and society. But some really isn't, and that is what I got to thinking about and ruminating over.

When I was a child, in the third grade, somebody stole a dollar from a coat pocket in the cloakroom. The teacher stood up before the class. She was an amazingly large woman as I recall. Or perhaps it was simply that I was small, and there were such great distances to look up to every grown person. She had three distinct chins, though, I'm sure of that.

"Who took Marilee's dollar?" she asked. Her tone was somber, heavy, hurt, surprised, and sharply accusing. "Raise your hand," she commanded. Everybody's hands stayed under everybody's desks. It went on for a very long time.

After a while my right arm began to twitch. After another while, my whole arm began to ache from holding it still against its will. Finally, in a moment of agony and heat, my arm shot up and my hand flapped at the end of it. I wanted to die. There was a big to-do. There were gasps, and the teacher's words swirling around and around, and my heart going so loud I couldn't hear them.

She put me in the back row. I was to see the principal the first thing after lunch! A note was to be sent home. Where was the dollar? I might even be expelled.

During the lunch recess the girl who owned the coat found the dollar down in the bottom of the torn lining. There was another to-do. Nobody could understand why I had raised my hand. I, who had never been known to have taken so much as a piece of candy from my mother's box without asking permission. I asked myself the same question. It stayed with me. When I was ten. When I was sixteen. And now again as I recall it.

Why did I feel guilty for something I hadn't done? I believe now that I acknowledged that theft I hadn't committed because there was something in me that *would have* committed a theft—if there wasn't something else in me that *wouldn't have* allowed it. That sounds confused, doesn't it? It really isn't. The good was there. The bad was there. The good knew it wouldn't steal the dollar. The bad knew it would if the good ever looked the other way. And I raised my hand in an unconscious gesture that recognized the existence of the bad.

There are times, and I believe now is one of them, when we

feel guilty for all the things we don't allow ourselves to do. The things we don't permit ourselves to think. The emotions we refuse to release in violence in this terribly violent present world.

It's most often the sins of omission that worry and fret at that subconscious. How do we, as Americans, feel about the fact that nobody has dropped an atom bomb except us? How do we feel when we hear of starving children all around the world? When we read about riots, see any injustice, read about any cruelty, come up against any callousness toward human life and human spirit? Do we want to raise our hand and say, "I did it. I contributed."

That's guilt. One kind of guilt. The realization that the weaknesses and meannesses of all humanity sneak their way into us just because we, too, are human. It's evil in a way, and dangerous. But it's something, I think, that perhaps once a year we should look right in the face. And ask ourselves a few very pertinent questions.

Does it have to go on, this guilt? Or can we study harder about whom to vote for, send a little money to help children we don't know at all, fight this pornographic bit in books and movies that we now just cluck over? Oh, even though we're only *one*, if this sort of member-of-the-human-race-guilt niggles at us enough, there's a great long number of things we can do.

ৰ্জ 56 ছ৵

SOCIAL LIFE

You know what? Sometimes I think that most modern homes are sort of a social disaster. It's a merry-go-round that spins off in tangents. It is held only by the home base in the middle, a place to eat, sleep, and change clothes.

121

You know how it is. Sally is off to her activities. Jackie is off to his. Dad has his own social life. You have yours. Where, I ask you, is the *home*?

I remember social life when I was very small. I remember a night when my mother and father and I went to a nearby small town on the street car, a long ride. It was a small home, too. But there were four couples and six assorted children.

The hostess was German. The bubbling smells from the top of her stove and the deep brown, rich colors from her oven are with me yet. The table was stretched to the length of a bridge and took three tablecloths. There was china. There was silver plate. But there wasn't any room at all for flowers and trimming because the great steaming platters of food covered every free inch.

As children, we sat together at the foot of the table. As children, we were served last. But there was plenty. We all groaned like the table when the feast was over. The women corralled our help for clearing. Then we were free while they took over the dish washing. Their voices rose and fell with the chink and clink and sudsy sound.

We ran through the backyard and around the front porch where the men sat with cigars. When the light of day quieted itself, the sound of the upright piano brought us all indoors. The small parlor was filled with the sound of "Shine on Harvest Moon," "Kathleen," "Sweet Adeline," "Wait Till the Sun Shines, Nelly."

When the repertoire and the voices were exhausted, we were put to bed. Our shoes off, we curled up all over the place. On the narrow, scratchy horsehair sofa, in the big cracked leather chair, on the floor before the fire. The living-room lights went out and the grown-ups headed for the dining-room table. Shafted and colored, the lamps from the other room and the old-fashioned green chandelier moved in slow patterns upon us, stilled our whispering and giggles to a half sleep.

It was weird and wonderful, that semislumber. We half

heard the hum of the women's voices, the secure con-trapuntal thump and rumble of the men's. You couldn't be a child in that darkened room, listening and partly hearing, without feeling loved, feeling safe.

It is the laughter I remember best, though. The game was Flinch, and they all were demon players. The laughter, the mirth, the drollery, lifted to the ceilings and fitted the walls like the paper on them.

I was always very happy in that town, in that small house and in all the other small houses of my family's friends. Leaning against my father, eyes closed, head nodding during the long streetcar ride home, the clack of the wheels on the metal rails was overlaid with laughter. The jounce of my father's shoulder as he carried me like a sack on the dark, late walk from the trolley to my bed took the rhythm of laughter and held it through my whole night's sleep.

People do not laugh much nowadays. They do not gather around pianos and sing. Flinch is a game long gone, perhaps not even remembered. Children do not climb haystacks on farms after a Sunday dinner for a half dozen families, or dress up and present little plays for the assembled and patient grown-ups while waiting for supper. There are baby-sitters now. There is what sometimes seems like a compulsive need for grown-ups to seek all entertainment *away* from their children as often as humanly possible. In an odd, intangible way, children are being rejected, in an important way, one they can sense, one that affects them and seems like in-difference to them, even if they don't know the word.

Yet, your friends have children. You have children. Your husband knows people. You know people. Your kids know other parents as well as other young people.

Do we have to seek, all of us, separate social lives, distant from each other? There can be, in a bringing together of all of these shared personalities, a new sort of cohesive social relationship for us all as a family.

Maybe it will take a while. Seem like a lot of trouble to

have children too. Some of your friends may even feel a little hampered in their freedom of speech and action with children around. But it can be done. It can be fun. It can be a real party in the true sense.

❧ SO LONG, NOW ❧

If you were sitting before my fireplace now, this is the time I would excuse myself and go out into the kitchen to put the kettle on for tea and arrange the cookies on my best milk glass platter.

But, of course, I cannot ask you into my home and know you and have you know me—in a fullness that is free of embarrassment and filled with a sense of timelessness.

I cannot do that. But I can thank you for coming to this little book in which I have written all the things I cannot say. Not to you, not to those who are nearest and dearest to me.

And I am grateful to you.